# Global Market Entry

# Global Market Entry

*Rules of Engagement*

Christopher Nagel

**To order additional copies of this book, contact:**
Xlibris Corporation
1-888-795-4274
www.Xlibris.com
Orders@Xlibris.com
117967

# Contents

*Dedication*
*for Molly, Jonathan and James*

# *Preface*

This volume is intended to assist managers newly assigned to meaningful international responsibilities—those with established positions, but looking for a primer on market-entry strategies, trade documentation, and the protection of a firm's international cash position.

This short pragmatic global text provides assistance on strategic decisions as well as serving as a reference for the more 'granular' issues of financial instruments.

A recommended approach to this text is to imagine that you, the reader, currently work for a division of a growing company and have been brought into a strategy meeting with a senior vice president. In that meeting, you are reassigned and tasked with devising and executing a plan to expand offshore revenues. You now face one of the most challenging, yet engaging, opportunities of your career. While you welcome the new assignment, you wonder how you should proceed.

Many fundamental decisions on how best to access and serve new markets need to be taken. As a lead manager, you must now decide *which* countries the firm should enter and in what sequence—and what criteria should be used to select those markets: proximity, stage of development, geographic region, cultural and legal issues, and the competitive situation. And then, *how* should your firm enter those new markets? Should it do so on an export basis using agents or distributors, or perhaps through entering into a JV (joint venture), or acquiring an established in-country firm, or more directly via a greenfield expansion?

This short book addresses key questions that global mangers face and examines strategies that a company can implement to 'go international'—starting with exporting and advancing all the way to a full-blown FDI (foreign direct investment). These options are not mutually exclusive and can be blended to improve both market access and a firm's competitive position.

The focus is on how you, the lead manager, can best decide to access offshore markets and position your company for long-term sustainable profitability.

Finally, and importantly, this executive primer concludes with perspectives on both the resurgence of China and on corporate ethics. These are two vital factors in world trade that all global managers must understand.

Numerous friends have given me the benefit of their knowledge on particular points, and my hearty thanks are due them. Enjoy the read.

# Chapter 1

## Going Global and Global Scale

Globalization is upon us. Those that embrace this reality will thrive. Those that think a domestic mindset is enough to be competitive will soon be obsolete.

Globalization is the at times controversial trend toward greater integration and interdependence of the world's economies—the increasing flow of goods, services, people, ideas, and people across borders.

Remarkably, between production and consumption, over 30% of the world's output of goods and services today cross a national border. This is 10% more than in the mid-1990s and double the pre-globalization ratio of the mid-1970s.[1] The trend will only continue. Supporters of globalization note the increased per capita income, standards of living and efficiency in all participating nations. Some correctly note that the benefits can be uneven, but we should not begrudge the improved standards of living of the hundreds of millions of workers in India, China, and elsewhere that came from embracing the rigors of the marketplace and participation in global trade.

Historically, given the size of the US domestic market, US producers have not 'needed' to be as engaged in global trade as smaller economies have, and so the US ranks a modest 35th in global engagement.[2] However, for growth (and indeed survival), US firms are moving to ever increasing participation in global trade. Today, leading US companies, such as Dow Chemical, 3M, General Electric, Intel, IBM, and McDonald's secure the majority of their revenues outside the US.

While the US is a major exporter, other countries are more integrated into the world economy. Exports account for 11% of GDP in the United

States, a healthy level, but much less than the 48% of GDP in Germany or the 70% of GDP in Taiwan. In fact, US exports as a percent of GDP are well below nearly all of the US major trading partners. While the US economy will grow at modest levels, the more significant economic growth will be offshore. Therefore those companies that position themselves to participate in this growth will outperform their domestic brethren.

The basic drivers of globalization are:

- Declining barriers to investment and trade (lower tariffs and quotas)
- Advances in technology and communications
- Changing consumer attitudes that are receptive to a world culture and global brands

Within these, the role of better transportation and communication systems has led to new and improved processes of high-volume production that, for the first time in history, enable substantial economies of scale sufficient to be called *global scale*. To benefit from the cost advantages of scale, globally-minded companies:

- Invest in production plants large enough to exploit a technology's potential economies of scale.
- Invest in global marketing and distribution networks so that sales volumes can keep pace with the new volume of production; a company's own sales force becomes the most dependable instrument for obtaining and holding market share large enough to ensure the cost advantages of scale.
- Invest in globally-capable management.

As noted by Harvard's A.D. Chandler, "This three-pronged investment in production, distribution, and management brought the modern [global] industrial enterprise into being." Such firms, "no longer competed primarily on the basis of price. Instead they competed for market share and profits through functional and strategic effectiveness. They did so *functionally* by improving their product, their processes of production, their marketing, their purchasing, and their labor relations, and *strategically* in becoming multinational by moving into growing markets more rapidly, and out of declining ones more quickly and effectively, than their competitors." Managers invested in new units of production and distribution to: ensure access to markets and supplies, prevent competitors from obtaining such access, improve the firm's overall tax position, and/or extend their firm's portfolio of revenue streams.

An excellent way to give context to 'going global' is to use real-world examples of the management decision process. For example, we will use the entry by International Paper Co. (the world's largest paper company) into the Asian beverage markets, and specifically the moves by its consumer packaging division, a producer of the familiar paper carton we see in retail stores for juice and milk. Despite its global sounding name, IP remains primarily focused on the North American market. So it is instructive to look at the 'why' behind IP's strategic moves in Asia—exporting to some countries and establishing greenfields (constructing physical plants) in others. The issues faced are not unique to IP and apply to a broad range of industries.

This text will show the various market approaches used by IP for market entry. The challenges faced by the company illustrate the breadth of issues that managers need to think through before 'going global.'

At a foundation level, we should also view IP's experience in the context of what has become known as 'new trade theory' as described by Paul Krugman, the 2008 Nobel Laureate. Krugman builds upon the classic trade theory in David Ricardo's *Principles of Political Economy.* Ricardo recognized that if a country specializes in producing that which it makes with comparative advantage (efficiency), and then trades those products for other goods that another country produces relatively efficiently, then both countries will benefit from the transaction; both countries' levels of consumption and standards of living will improve. Krugman notes, "The theory of comparative advantage is alive and well, but has lost some of its monopoly position." He observes that the ongoing expansion in world trade has enabled both specialization and large-scale production. He stresses that "increasing returns" (what managers call economies of scale) are a major complement to the opening of markets, the increase in world trade and the growth of the multinational corporation.

Large scale production plus specialization means that goods and services can be produced at a lower cost when made in volume via more efficient production runs. Such production provides both lower prices and a diversity of products for the global consumer. Small-scale production for local markets is replaced by large-scale production for global markets (again, referred to as global scale).

Alongside global scale, an important competitive factor is what our Economics brethren term 'first-mover' advantage. Here firms that make early (and major) investments in global scale plants achieve the key competitive advantage of low-cost production, enabling higher profitability over lesser-volume competitors, plus the ability to amortize other fixed investments, such as R&D and advertising, over an increased number of units. First-mover advantage raises both high capital and market barriers for competitors contemplating entering an industry, which can result in an industry led by a few very strong multinationals. The term first-mover in marketing also applies to geography, where a firm that positions itself first in a market overseas can establish such a strong market position that it will preclude all but the strongest competitors' entry. Unlike classic trade theory, which dismisses the role of governments as an impediment to efficiency, we should note that new trade theory adds the perspective that national governments can and do play a beneficial role in a nation's competitiveness via encouraging nascent technologies and industries and so provide a basis for future scale and competitive advantage.[3]

As companies grow, managers increasingly appreciate the value of positioning their firms to maximize market share, not only in the home market, but also in the world market. Success in global markets naturally increases a firm's total volumes, while lowering its cost position both domestically and abroad.

## Case Study—International Paper

The factors of economies of scale, specialization and first-mover advantage led IP to invest in global scale paper mills. These mills, coupled with IP's vertically-integrated access to timberlands and an efficient logistics infrastructure, positioned IP to achieve a sustained competitive advantage.

IP's paper mills were sized to serve the market needs of its regional US converting plants (i.e., those that 'convert' large roll stock into the actual cartons used by dairy and juice processors), plus additional capacity to produce and export commodity roll-stock to other modern paper converters in the advanced economies of Europe and Japan. IP's principal markets for roll-stock were in what is known as *The Triad*, the leading economies of Western Europe, North America and Japan.

However, markets are not static; markets evolve. Despite its strong competitive cost position, IP's paper operations were put in jeopardy in its home market by the growing use of the now ubiquitous plastic gallon milk jug. Consumers that had once purchased milk in quarts and half-gallons increasingly began to buy milk by the gallon, and plastic jugs presented a lower cost and more convenient option to milk processors than traditional paper. Today, plastic jugs have all but replaced the paper gallon carton and continue to take share from half-gallon paper, though less so in the high-margin juice and juice-drink category where paper's superior printability and 'billboarding' hold a market benefit over plastic, and is beneficially used by such brands as Coca Cola's *Minute Maid* and Pepsico's *Tropicana*. The reader may recognize that such a market challenge reflects one of Michael Porter's 'Five Forces'—the threat of substitute products.

With the loss of market volumes to plastic, IP's primary paper mills began operating below design level, a critical underutilization of fixed capital assets (note: a global-scale paper mill represents a sunk cost of $1 billion each). Senior managers of capital intensive industries like steel and paper fully appreciate the relationship between cost and volume and the penalties of operating below design efficiency.

Capital intensive firms use the accounting concept of 'over and under absorbed burden' to track and manage costs. If a paper mill operates below standard volumes (based on anticipated market size and design capacity), this loss is listed as 'under absorbed burden'; if the mill operates above the standard volume, the resulting gain is listed as 'over absorbed burden.' Over and under absorbed burdens are key to asset utilization at each mill, and, indeed, to the profitability of IP as a whole.

The plastic jug's success in taking share from paper put the paper mills' low cost position and profitability in jeopardy. To preserve economies of scale, IP recognized it had to expand its presence offshore and so compensate for its flat and eroding domestic volumes. 'Going international' and generating increased export volumes would not only help return the primary paper mills to efficient scale, but those offshore volumes would concurrently improve the allocation of fixed costs per unit, and thus help preserve the company's existing domestic market position and profitability. Per Chandler above, the loss of share to a competitor not only increases production costs, but also decreases those of one's competitor. He further notes that the new capital intensive industries can no longer afford to depend upon commercial intermediaries who make their profits by handling products of more than one manufacturer. Manufacturers (like IP) need a sales force to concentrate full-time on advertising, canvassing for customers, assuring delivery on schedule, providing installation, service and repair, and customer credit.

IP took the decision to move beyond 'passive' exporting of commodity paper board to paper companies in Europe and Japan and become actively involved in growing consumer demand for modern paper packaging, specifically in the Asian markets. Beyond the commodity margins of bulk roll stock, IP looked to capture healthy value-added margins by selling finished cartons directly to local beverage companies. To fulfill this strategic goal, IP managers knew the company had to forward-integrate and establish production inside the major Asian markets and there convert bulk roll stock into high-quality, ready-to-fill printed cartons. IP then assembled a team of international marketers to take the company into the key Asian markets. For a further marketing edge and to leverage in-house expertise, the team was tasked also with setting up regional support staffs to provide local dairy and juice processors with technical assistance and in-country marketing support.

So the 'why' of IP going international in Asia was a combination of an operational push from domestic operations (as a result of the loss of home market share), the pull of market opportunities beyond the home market, and the inherent value of diversifying one's revenue sources. How IP's global staff managed the market entry into the markets of Japan, South Korea and Taiwan will be discussed later.

## Market Criteria for International Business, and Creating a Short-list

The decision to engage in export marketing should naturally be based on potential market size, competitor activities, and overall marketing issues. Your firm will not have the management 'bandwidth' to enter all markets at once, so you will need to develop a short list of one or more markets to target and enter.

To assist this process, and before proceeding internationally with sourcing, exporting, or investing, a manager must first look at the broad market conditions in the prospective overseas markets and analyze what the advantages, disadvantages, and costs will be. Managers should review several basic areas:

**#1, Political Risk and Data Analysis** Political risk is the risk of a change in government policy that would adversely impact a company's ability to operate effectively and profitably. This is a concern and deterrent in expanding internationally. Political risk includes possible future issues of currency convertibility, expropriation and even political violence. The lower the level of political risk, the more likely a company will invest in that country or market. The difficulty of assessing political risk is inversely proportional to a country's stage of economic development. The political risk of the Triad countries, for example, is quite limited, compared to less developed preindustrial countries in Africa, Latin America, or Asia. Firms new to international business should appreciate that over 80% of all exports from the US are to just 25 countries, representing the Triad or the 'Economic Tigers' of Asia (Taiwan, South Korea, Singapore and Hong Kong) plus several of the major oil producing states (Saudi Arabia, the UAE).[4]

To improve the chance of success, a prudent manager may wish to focus initial market development in these 25 markets, as they represent high income markets with a lower level of political risk, and are well integrated into the world economy. Less advanced smaller economies present second-tier opportunities that may well require greater investment in market resources and longer timelines for financial returns. Beyond the Triad and the Tigers, managers need to decide the sequence of markets to be seriously considered for market development and entry.

To help managers 'filter' markets, the World Bank has a useful online resource called *Doing Business*. This ranks 183 countries on such issues as the Ease of Doing Business, Trading Across Borders and Protecting Investors. Fortunately, with the exception of a few countries like Venezuela, managers today face a lower risk of expropriation of their foreign operations. Most nations now recognize the benefits of privatization, foreign investment, and the wide-spread failure of SOEs (state owned enterprises). Also, as national economies are increasingly integrated into the world economy, members of the EU, OECD and the WTO are more likely to abide by international norms with resulting reduced political risk. Nonetheless, and beyond the globally integrated economies, if a manager wishes to establish operations in a second-tier economy, she may elect to protect her firm against the political risks of currency inconvertibility, expropriation, destruction due to civil unrest or political instability, by purchasing political risk insurance from OPIC (the Overseas Private Investment Corporation). This is a self-sustaining US agency with the enlightened goal of promoting US investment in developing countries. MNCs (Multinational Corporations) can incorporate political risk insurance premiums into the capital budgeting process and adjust a project's NPV (net present value) by reducing future cash flows by the OPIC premium.

Naturally, 'going international' is more efficient when the local political environment is transparent and relatively free of corruption. To assist in developing the sequence of overseas markets to enter, marketers should also review the country rankings of Berlin-based Transparency International. This group has developed a *Corruption Perceptions Index* that gauges levels of public sector corruption in 180 countries and territories. Less corruption means less 'non-scientific' costs and fewer barriers to market efficiency.

Much specific market data is available online, including websites maintained by trade authorities of individual countries. Whatever the source of information, a manager's goal must be to understand the major factors that will affect demand for a product or service. National income data is a good starting point on which to base demand estimates and guide the sequence in which markets are ranked and developed. However, we should add the caveat that macro-data tells only part of any story.

For example, India, one of the high-growth BRIC (Brazil, Russia, India, China) countries, has a population of close to 1.2 billion people. As recently as 1985, more than 90% of Indians lived on less than a dollar a day, so this would seem to be an unattractive market. However, in the current generation, GDP/capita has risen to US$3,700 PPP (meaning purchasing power parity). While this may still seem a relatively modest level, the McKinsey Global Institute reports that 5% of Indian society is in fact middle class and able to afford most consumer goods. For any marketer, an educated and increasingly affluent market of 50 million customers (a population greater than that of the Western States of California, Oregon, and Washington combined) should not be ignored. McKinsey further forecasts that within two decades, 40% of India's population (583 million people) will have middle class status. Spending patterns will grow rapidly on discretionary items ranging from personal products to packaged foods and consumer electronics. And India will surpass Germany as the world's fifth-largest consumer economy.[5]

Thus 'unpacking' summary data is important. Another example of getting behind summary data is Angola. This is a leading African oil exporter, a member of OPEC, and a country with a GDP/capita of US$5,900 PPP. Angola would seem to present a more attractive and affluent market than India. However, Angola has just 1% of India's population, two-thirds of which survive on less than $2 per day. Angola ranks near the bottom of almost every United Nations HDI (Human Development Index) with an average life expectancy of just 38 years and a deserved reputation for pervasive corruption.[6] There are surely more promising markets to investigate and enter. Again, unpacking the numbers can be illuminating and the easy perception that any wealthy OPEC oil state should offer a favorable consumer market doesn't pass scrutiny.

Some useful online sources:

| | |
|---|---|
| World Bank: | http://www.doingbusiness.org/ |
| OPIC: | http://www.opic.gov/ |
| Transparency Int'l: | http://www.transparency.org/ |

**#2, Market Access** Another factor in selling into a market or establishing offshore production is market access. In the case of Japan, in-country distribution is so complicated that foreign companies will not succeed without entering into a close relationship or partnership with a local distributor. For example, capable global firms like Tropicana and Bristol-Myers Squibb do not even try to self-distribute in Japan, but have built partnerships within the local supply-chain. In some countries, the better distributors may already be 'taken' by competitors and your firm may in fact be faced with very restricted or no market access. Also, if a country constrains market access by limiting imports, it may become necessary to establish a production facility within the country itself.

An example of access is the Japanese automobile firms locating production facilities in America. Given US political concerns in the 1980s regarding the major market gains by Japanese imports and the resultant imposition of 'voluntary' restraints, Japanese auto companies invested in US plant capacity because of concerns about sustained market access. By producing cars in the US, they are able to supply the lucrative US automobile market while not being exposed to the ongoing threat of US tariffs or quotas. Similarly, US companies continue to create production capacity abroad to ensure continued access to markets that had initially been established with exports from US-based plants.

Additional issues for managers to research are the levels of import duties and non-tariff barriers (e.g., quotas, inspection rules, and certificates, etc.—all known as NTBs). Care also should be taken to understand foreign exchange and cross-border payment controls and any import/export license protocols. Such information is country-specific and can be accessed via contacting the consulates or trade bureaus of those countries under consideration. One's own country's overseas-based commercial attachés can provide a range of background information, including introductions to potential local agents or distributors.

**#3, *Economic Factor Costs*** Factor costs are land, labor, and capital. Of these, a key is often the compensation costs of workers, especially in manufacturing. Hourly labor rates (in US dollars) range from just $0.61/ hour in Sri Lanka to $1.36/hour in China, $6.23 in Mexico, $19.10/hour in Singapore and $16.62/hour in South Korea. European labor costs in manufacturing are broadly higher than those in the US. For example, Bureau of Labor Statistics data on hourly labor costs show the US at $34.74/hour compared to $43.76/hour in Germany and to a European high of $57.53/ hour in Norway.[7] Managers should incorporate such comparative data in their country and market analyses.

Another word of caution. Such data sets are useful, but do have their limitations. Given the size of the US economy and that world trade is often reported/denominated in US dollars, local compensation costs are frequently converted to a US dollar basis and used as indicators of competitiveness of manufactured goods in world trade. This is a useful benchmark, but one needs to factor-in such issues as the appreciation of the Euro against the US dollar, which can and has resulted in apparent double-digit increases in European labor costs (in US$ terms) that do not reflect the more modest actual increases in local currency (€). Similarly, an undervalued Chinese Yuan vis-à-vis the US$ provides a challenge to comparative analysis.

While comparative labor costs are useful in deciding where to locate off-shore production/assembly, the data also should be put to use in gauging the buying power of workers in an overseas economy, and so assist managers in determining which markets present the greatest in-market sales opportunities. As part of the process of determining which overseas markets to pursue, managers can review country-to-country comparisons developed by the UN, especially the HDI (Human Development Index) that provides data and comparative rankings of 180 countries on such macro-development issues as Adult Literacy, Life Expectancy, and GDP/capita PPP.

Moreover, while wage levels are important, they are only one of the costs of production and, in capital-intensive industries, are often only a small percentage of the total costs associated with a product. Global managers are known to follow a general rule that when wage costs are less than 15% of a product's total cost, wage rates become a secondary factor in competitiveness. The application by MNCs of advanced computer controls and manufacturing technologies has reduced the proportion of labor relative to capital in many industries. Thus, in formulating a sourcing strategy, company managers should recognize the declining importance of direct manufacturing labor as a percentage of total product costs.

The better managed global companies do not blindly chase cheap labor for manufacturing locations, exactly because direct labor may well be a small percentage of total costs. Therefore, it may not be worthwhile to incur the costs and risks of establishing manufacturing activity in distant locations. Senior managers are also mindful of the associated 'opportunity cost' of allocating scarce and costly management time to a headlong race to find the lowest labor costs, while the other factors of production, land, materials, and capital may be more important. The cost of such factors depends on their availability and relative abundance. Often, between the major industrialized countries, the differences in factor costs offset each other so that, on balance, companies have a 'level field' in the competitive arena. When this is the case, the critical factors become management and worker effectiveness, i.e., productivity.

Beyond the industrialized economies of the Triad, there is a second tier of industrializing countries—for example Malaysia and other Pacific Rim countries—that offer significant factor cost savings, increasingly developed infrastructure, and political stability. These are often attractive manufacturing and market locations. A third tier includes Russia and other countries that have not yet become significant locations for manufacturing activity. As noted, low factor costs (especially wages) can be offset by limited infrastructure, lower levels of development (per the HDI) and greater political uncertainty.

The proximity of production to the end-user is often important and, in general, the greater the distance between product manufacture and the target market, the greater the time-delay for delivery and the cost of transportation. However, in what some call the 'death of distance,' innovative transportation technologies continue to cut both transportation time and expense. For example, through using design-built ocean vessels (specifically PCC 'pure car carrier' ships that can load 10,000 cars), the cost of transporting a car from South Korea to the Port of Baltimore is no more expensive than overland delivery of a car from Detroit. So also in logistics, we see the major beneficial impact of scale economies.[8]

Manufacturers today take full advantage of *intermodal* services that allow the now ubiquitous 40' shipping container to be readily transferred between truck, rail and ocean carriers. A container can be securely loaded and sealed at an exporter's loading dock, hauled by truck or train to the port of embarkation, loaded on an ocean carrier and shipped to the port of discharge where it is off-loaded and similarly moved by truck or train to the consignee's own inland factory and loading dock. In its own quiet way, containerization and thus standardization of freight has revolutionized shipping and greatly enabled the expansion of global trade. We also note that in Europe with the advent of the single EU market, the removal of border controls has further sped up delivery times and lowered costs.

*#4, Country Infrastructure* In order to present an attractive setting for a manufacturing operation, a country's infrastructure should be sufficiently developed to support a modern operation. The specific infrastructure needs will vary from company to company, but minimally will include power, transportation, communications, service and component suppliers, a literate labor pool, civil order, and competent governance. In addition, unless a

company is already capable of handling barter and issues of countertrade, the prospective country should offer ready access to foreign exchange for the purchase of material and components from abroad, plus the ability to accommodate the repatriation of profits, fees and intra-company transfer payments.

Countries with cheap labor may have neither the necessary support services nor infrastructure to support a manufacturing activity. Among the challenges of doing business in the Indian and Russian markets is that infrastructure is often unable to handle an increased volume of shipments.

A brief word on the BRIC, an acronym coined by Goldman-Sachs in 2001 to represent the major growth markets of Brazil, Russia, India and China. An interesting comment by Goldman's Ed Forst is that Russia hasn't lived up to its growth potential, due to the non-adoption of market mechanisms, the rise of the oligarchs, and endemic corruption and violence, so that Russia in the BRIC should now be spelled with a lower case 'r'. More recently, Goldman has coined the term the N-11, i.e., the 'next eleven' largest population markets after the BRIC, which, with evolving economic and political conditions, will greatly impact the global economy. The N-11 includes Bangladesh, Egypt, Indonesia, Iran, Korea, Mexico, Nigeria, Pakistan, Philippines, Turkey and Vietnam No one is saying business in all these markets is easy, but they are worth first-mover consideration alongside the benefit of diversifying revenue streams. Note: Goldman's N-11 fund does not invest in Iran.

***#5, Foreign Exchange*** In deciding where to locate a manufacturing activity, the costs of production and levels of profitability will be determined in part by the prevailing foreign exchange rate for the country's currency. Exchange rates can be volatile. Many companies pursue global sourcing strategies from a 'portfolio' of countries and in a range of currencies as a way of limiting exchange-related risk. At any point in time, what had been an attractive location for sales or production may become much less attractive due to exchange rate fluctuations. The prudent company will incorporate exchange volatility into its planning assumptions and be prepared to prosper under a variety of exchange rate relationships.

Dramatic shifts in price levels of commodities and currencies are a characteristic of the world economy. Such volatility argues for a sourcing strategy that provides alternative country options for supplying markets. Thus, for example, if at some time the US dollar($), the Yen(¥), the

Euro(€) or the Korean Won become seriously overvalued, a company with productive capacity in other 'currency locations' can achieve competitive advantage by shifting production among sites.

## *Ranking Market Opportunities*

With the above as a foundation, your next step is to make a short list and then decide which market(s) to enter. This decision is one that will determine the trajectory of your career (no pressure).

If your company is getting into exporting for the first time, its perspective will understandably reflect its experience in its home market. Global markets are highly competitive. So take time and think this through.

Managers must remember the classic truth in marketing that if a firm wants to penetrate an existing market, it must offer more value than its competitors—sounds easy—but isn't. Managers should take to heart the approach expressed by Harvard's Michael Porter on three core competitive strategies from which to choose and pursue: *cost leadership, differentiation,* and *niche focus.* Unfortunately, some firms don't develop and stick to a clear strategy and try to be good on all strategic counts, and end up being good at none.[9]

Also, to quote GE's legendary CEO Jack Welch, "If you don't have a competitive advantage, don't compete." Marketing managers must look to not only meet customer expectations, but also must strive to exceed them. This naturally applies as much to export marketing as marketing at home. And recall that most consumer product launches fail—so managers should position their firms for the greatest chance of success.

Alongside reviewing the 25 countries that represent over 80% of all US exports, a useful market selection approach to consider can be 'marketing by analogy.' If the market characteristics of a prospective market are similar to those where your firm already operates, such a market can be investigated and pursued with some level of confidence.

As an example, International Paper had developed a shelf-stable (not requiring refrigeration) juice package for Nestlé-Panama. An operational benefit for Nestlé was that the carton's packaging line could be readily added alongside their traditional canning operation with minimal capital expense or disruption. A market benefit was broader access to retail shelf-space for its *Libby's* brand. With this business up and running, IP then looked to expand such systems into other countries. Using marketing by analogy, IP looked for markets similar to Panama's, i.e., markets with a hot tropical climate, a literate largely urban society, an entrepôt trading tradition, one open to foreign technology and brands, with capable local distribution, but where there was limited refrigeration space in consumers' homes. One market with these same (analogous) characteristics is Hong Kong, a market that IP was then supplying with other products, but not yet the innovative juice carton. IP marketers then worked with a leading Hong Kong supermarket chain to install a processing and packaging line to roll-out juice drinks in the new IP packaging under the local supermarket's licensed *Sunkist* brand.

As a lead manager, you will need to gauge the longer term market potential for your firm's products. If there is a range of likely prospective markets, you should try early-on to rank those markets' potential profitability and tighten the focus onto those markets with true potential. This so you will not divert limited and high cost management time on lesser prospect 'also ran' markets.

Mangers will need to ask what are the needs for product modification and export packing. And managers will need to understand shipping costs and order fulfillment needs (the time from order receipt to physical delivery in-country). Shipping costs will naturally affect the attractiveness of a specific product in an offshore market. If a firm's export product is similar to what is already being manufactured inside the target market, shipping costs, duties and 'time on the water' may render the exported product non-competitive. Thus, managers need to understand logistics and always look for ways to differentiate their products in the market. Your firm, as an exporter, may need to offset a local competitive price or delivery disadvantage. The issue of local in-country production, whether by one's own company or a competitor, is a key competitive question.

Another crucial step that cannot be overstressed is the need to visit the potential market(s). Once you have your prospective markets pared down to a short-list, there is simply no substitute for being 'on the ground' to get a real-world sense of a market's potential and the stage an imported product would fit in the local product and market life-cycle. A market visit should do several things. It should confirm (or contradict) assumptions regarding market potential. It should provide the necessary yet non-quantifiable 'atmospherics' for management judgment. And the visit or series of visits should be used to gather any additional data necessary to reach a final go/no-go decision.

A good way to gauge a potential market is to attend a trade show in-country. Trade fairs, usually organized around a product or industry, are held in major markets overseas. For assistance with trade events and trade missions, good support can be found at the online ITA portal at: http://www.trade.gov.

By attending trade shows or participating in trade missions, you can conduct assessments on developing or expanding markets, find distributors or agents, and locate potential end users. Through attending trade shows, marketers can learn a great deal about competitors' technology, pricing, and the depth of their market penetration. Overall, you should be able to get a good general impression of competitors in a target market while at the same time promoting your own products and services.

### *Market Expansion Strategies—major alternatives*

With full credit to the formative work of professors Igal Ayal and Jehiel Zif, and the textbook extension by Warren Keegan, lead managers should consider two major strategies in expanding international operations:

*market segment concentration vs. diversification*
and
*country concentration vs. diversification*

With these, managers will need to make judgments on whether to:

- expand by pursuing new markets segments in countries where one's firm already does business or
- pursue new country markets for a firm's existing/familiar market segments

These two strategies lead authors Ayal & Zif to give the four options shown here: [10]

*Market Expansion Strategies Based on Countries and Segments*

|  | Segment Concentration | Segment Diversification |
|---|---|---|
| Country Concentration | #1, Narrow focus | #2, Country focus |
| Country Diversification | #3, Country Diversification | #4, Global Diversification |

In Strategy #1, a firm concentrates on a few market segments in just a few countries. This is a reasonable starting point for firms new to export.

In Strategy #2, a firm has country concentration but market segment diversification, where a company looks to serve a range of markets in a few countries. According to US Export Data, approximately 58% of American exporters sell to just one foreign country while 25% of US exporters ship to two-to-four countries. Thus, together, 83% of US exporting firms have sales to four or fewer countries, and so we see the majority of US exporters following a concentrated market approach and pursuing Strategy #1 or Strategy #2.

In Strategy #3, capable multinational firms look for country diversification and market segment concentration, which is the strategy whereby a firm pursues world markets for a narrow mix of products (presumably where it has both core-competencies and a competitive advantage). The benefit of this strategy is that by serving the world customer, a firm can achieve greater scale, achieve lower costs than its competitors, and therefore approach having, in Keegan's words, "an unassailable competitive advantage." Strategy #3 firms represent large integrated, multiple-site operations and the bulk of US exports. Compared to the 83% of US firms in Strategy #1 or #2, the 17% of American firms that export to more than four countries represent nearly 90% of the value of all US exports. We should also note that the larger American exporting companies (those with 500+ employees) are responsible for over 66% of exports, yet represent only 2% of the number of exporting firms. Further, the data shows that over half of US exports, by value, are accounted for by just 250 US firms.[11]

In Strategy #4, truly global firms pursue both country diversification and segment diversification, the type of multi-business company embodied in the giant Japanese trading companies, the *sogo shosha*. Globally, such conglomerates are few, with General Electric perhaps the only US candidate. An example of a Japanese conglomerate is Mitsubishi, multi-country in scope with dozens of business groups serving multiple market segments (everything from consumer toaster ovens to bulk chemicals).

## *Strategies and Stages of Development*

We should now take a moment to reflect on the various stages in the evolution of the global corporation, from domestic to international, to multinational, and then to becoming truly global. The difference between a purely domestic firm and a Strategy #1 international company is simply that the international firm serves markets in other countries. Like the domestic company, it is often ethnocentric and home-country oriented. The Strategy #2 international company extends to new segment opportunities beyond the home country and develops marketing programs to exploit those opportunities. A major change in orientation occurs as a company moves to Strategy #3, multinational country diversification. At this point, the management perspective shifts significantly from ethnocentric to polycentric. The difference is important. While a Strategy #2 ethnocentric company may seek to extend its products and practices to foreign countries and looks for similarities outside its home market, it is probably less appreciative of market differences. The Strategy #3 multinational sees differences, not as problems to manage, but as important opportunities to expand market knowledge and exploit new opportunities.

A distinctive quality of a company moving from Strategy #3 to Strategy #4 is the pursuit of globally integrated strategies that include having key assets dispersed, specialized, and interdependent. A global automobile company, Toyota for example, makes engines and transmissions in various countries and ships these components to assembly plants located in each of the world regions. Specialized design labs are located in different countries yet work together on the same project. The role of in-country marketing changes dramatically as a company moves through the stages of development. In Strategies #1 and #2, the responsibility of the marketing organization is to realize the potential of individual national markets. In globally diversified firms, the responsibility of marketers is to not only realize the potential of each national market, but also contribute to the success of marketing efforts worldwide, by sharing successful innovations and ideas with the entire organization.

Each of the four Strategy stages has its strengths. The international company has the ability to exploit the parent company's knowledge and capabilities outside the home country. The multinational's strength is the ability to adapt and respond to national differences with local responsiveness. The global company leverages internal skills and resources by taking advantage of global markets and global resources. In consumer electronics, the Strategy #4 company Panasonic (formerly Matsushita) is able to serve global markets from world-scale plants and create very robust competition for Philips Electronics in the Netherlands and General Electric in the US. A globally diversified company combines the strengths of each of the strategic stages and serves global markets by accessing a breadth of global resources, and simultaneously leveraging its global learning and experience.

A cultural observation is that when a firm operates under Strategy #1 and #2, key jobs are mostly assigned to home-country nationals. Under Strategy #3, key jobs in host countries go increasingly to country nationals, though headquarters management positions are largely still held by home-country nationals. In Strategy #4, the best person is selected for management positions regardless of nationality. We note that the CEO of the Renault-Nissan Alliance is Brazilian-born Carlos Ghosn.

Finally, for a firm in Strategy #1 or #2, research and development (R&D) is largely conducted in the home country. But as firms move into Strategy #3 and #4, R&D becomes decentralized. Ultimately, when a company reaches true global diversification, R&D becomes just one part of a range of integrated and decentralized worldwide approaches to planning and operations.

With this foundational introduction to the global marketplace, we shall next look at the ways for you to successfully take your division international.

1   Steven Roach, Chief Economist Morgan Stanley, The Christian Science Monitor, 2007

2   KOF Index of Globalization, ETH, Zurich, 2012

3   This section draws on: *Scale and Scope*, A.D. Chandler, 1990; and *The Conscience of a Liberal*, Paul Krugman, 2008.

4   US Dept. of Commerce, A Profile of US Exporting Companies, release 2012

5   Diana Farrell and Eric Beinhocker, "Next Big Spenders: India's Middle Class," *BusinessWeek*, 5/19/07

6   *Oil glorious oil*, The Economist, 1/30/10

7   US Dept. of Labor, Bureau of Labor Statistics, International Comparisons of Hourly Compensation, release 2011

8   Maryland Port Administration

9   Michael Porter, *Competitive Strategy: Techniques for Analyzing Industries and Competitors*, 1980

10  Igal Ayal and Jeheil Zif, *Competitive Market Choice Strategies in Multinational Marketing*, Columbia Journal of World Business, 1978; and Warren Keegan, *Global Marketing Management*, 2002

11  US Department of Commerce, ibid.

# Chapter 2

## Global Entry

### How are you going to get there?

This chapter provides an overview of important issues, decisions, and steps necessary to succeed in global trade. While useful as a narrative, the chapter can also serve as a reference and guide.

A key issue that your expanding firm must address is whether to serve a select overseas market via exports from your home country (or from a third country if the firm is truly global) or to manufacture the product in the target country, or to do both, by initially serving and growing the market on an export-basis until investment in local production can be justified. This is a critical and far-reaching decision. In some emerging markets this may be a non-issue if local in-country production is required by that national government. However, in most high-income countries (e.g., Triad, Economic Tigers) and the NICs (newly industrialized countries), local production is not mandatory, so you must carefully choose your approach based upon the market and economic merits.

Assuming that you have the latitude to make the choice, you should review the trade-offs for the various options of local, regional, or global production. These include issues of direct costs, quality, delivery, and perceived customer value. Local costs naturally include labor, materials, capital, land, and transportation. As noted in the introductory section on globalization, scale economies are an important factor, and for every product there is a minimum volume level required to justify a capital investment. Naturally, from a pure market and service perspective, there is value and competitive advantage in being physically close to one's customers. Again, how you proceed is a far-reaching decision.

If you decide the best way to serve a market's needs is via local in-country production, you face the options of buying, building, or renting a manufacturing plant, or to cooperate with a local manufacturer in an arrangement called contract-manufacturing. In this case, an existing local manufacturer may be in a position to support incremental production (add a second shift, etc.) to their in-situ plant with less investment than the exporter would have to make to achieve the same level of output. Many factories do indeed have excess capacity, so adding 'throughput' to that fixed asset would be beneficial to that local firm and will likely induce the local manager to contract-manufacture at an attractive price.

As part of our ongoing case study on International Paper Company, we note that IP initially served dairy processors in South Korea and Taiwan via exports from an efficient converting plant in California. When those markets had reached a level to support in-country production, the investment decision was made to forward-integrate operations into those countries. While IP-domestic paid an economic penalty through reduced volumes (throughput), reduced efficiency, and less economies of scale at the California operation, management calculated this penalty would be more than offset by growth and profitability in those offshore market positions, as well as improve IP's competitive position versus firms still trying to sell those markets on an export basis.

## Export Marketing

We should note briefly that there is a difference between *export selling* and *export marketing*. Export selling involves minimal tailoring of the Four Ps (product, price, promotion, place) of the marketing mix to meet the needs of an offshore customer. The only marketing mix element that differs in export selling is place, i.e., the country where the product is sold and the logistics of getting it there. This selling approach can work for some products and services, especially those that are unique or for which there is minimal international competition. Companies new to exporting may initially experience some success with this. However, such an approach and managerial mind-set is increasingly inappropriate and ineffective. As companies mature and understand the global marketplace, and as global competitors expand operations, success requires that managers engage in true export marketing by tailoring the marketing mix elements to local market demands.

Exporting is a natural first step for a company to go international. We will later explore the other market access options of licensing, franchising, joint ventures, and FDI (foreign direct investment). There is a logical progression in moving to increasing levels of involvement in overseas markets, and, though any such order is not fixed (and some firms will bypass or omit various stages), the general sequence is:

We should note that each of these progressive levels of in-country presence can affect customer value perceptions, which in years past was often tied to a product's country of origin. If a market's consumers are nationalistic, they may prefer products made in their home country. However, the cachet of a non-local brand or product can actually be preferred if produced locally in partnership with a local firm and generates employment. Such preferences can be readily identified using market research. Today, with the rise of globalization, a product's country of origin is increasingly less important, so brand value and differentiation become critical.

---

- Indirect Export (via an Export Management Company)
- Direct Export (often with a local agent)
- Licensing/Franchising
- Joint Venture (a partially-owned FDI)
- Wholly-owned FDI
- Global Strategic Partnership

---

### *Comment on country of origin issues:*

While at times xenophobic, modern Japanese society displays a fascination with American music and culture. The runaway profitability of Disney-Tokyo reflects this trait as does the success of western-sounding labels in Japan. A remarkable marketing success was the Coca-Cola Company's launch of the *Georgia* brand of ready-to-drink (RTD) coffee, sold in Japan via the truly ubiquitous vending machine. While the State of Georgia is not exactly known for its coffee groves, it is an interesting 'American sounding' word. In a marketing masterstroke, Coca-Cola managers arranged for the late Ray Charles to travel to Japan to be the spokesperson for the product and sing the classic, *Georgia on my Mind*. Successful marketing in Japan is often tied to products that are perceived to be 'in vogue' and a great number of Japanese consumers connect themselves to the cachet of foreign products. Coffee (not tea, the main beverage in Japan) was thus sold with a foreign sounding brand name (*Georgia*) and the 'cool' foreign music of America. *Georgia* RTD coffee is sold via Coca-Cola's one million+ vending machines and is so successful that the machines carry an average of three slots each of *Georgia* coffee. The drink remains one of the most profitable products in Coca Cola's global portfolio.

Moving across the East China Sea from Japan into China, we see a market reality that many Chinese consumers view domestic brands as inferior, which is in part due to the legacy of poor quality consumer products from the era of SOEs (state-owned enterprises). Retail markets in China offer a wide range of global brand knock-offs such as Gucci and Louis Vuitton. The Chinese consumer will often prefer a domestically produced fake product carrying a foreign brand over a domestic product. As the president of Ogilvy-China has noted, "Everyone in China has religion in branding." [1]

Global companies benefit from leveraging their brands' equity and educating overseas customers on the value and quality benefits that a global brand (such as Bayer, IBM, Coca-Cola, Nestlé) represents. The brand itself becomes more important than the actual country of manufacture. Diversified global companies can often source products from multiple locations and customers increasingly trust the inherent quality of the brand and care less about the country of origin.

## *The Decision to Export*

A domestic company can 'go international' simply by responding to an unsolicited order that just shows up 'over the transom.' Regrettably, some companies may consider themselves too busy (!) or unable to respond to an overseas inquiry. A firm may respond but still operate in *domestic selling mode* by simply quoting off a pricelist and saying the customer is welcome to pick up the product anytime at the factory's loading dock. A more enterprising firm, one that makes a commitment to operating in the global arena by allocating funding and personnel, would view such an inquiry as an opportunity for market research and growth and something that offers the potential for a new, ongoing and meaningful revenue stream. The enterprising firm will also appreciate the role that exports can play in extending the application of a technology or a product's life cycle, especially if such sales are mature or declining domestically. While the probability of being an exporter does increase with a firm's size, many small and mid-size companies succeed with exports and a firm's 'export intensity' (the ratio of export sales to total sales) does not necessarily correlate with a company's size.

Beyond simply taking orders, export marketers should try to understand and approach target customers in the context of the total market environment. The capable export marketer does not just take a domestic product 'as is' and simply sell it to international customers. The product offered in the home market should be a starting point that is then modified to meet the range of preferences in overseas markets. Within the marketing mix, the export manager sets prices to fit a broader marketing strategy and should not merely extend home-country pricing to offshore customers. The incremental costs of export shipment preparation, transportation, and financing should be factored into the determination of prices, but pricing should always be *to market* and not at some arbitrary level decided by some internal cost accountant. And within the marketing mix, a wise export marketer will develop and implement strategies for communication, distribution and service that are tailored to specific markets.

Export marketing requires an understanding of the target market, the use of marketing research, and the calculation of market potential. These will inform decisions concerning product design, pricing, distribution, advertising, and communications, i.e., the marketing mix

While increased sales and profitability are the anticipated benefits of exporting, 'going international' also provides the advantage of increased flexibility in dealing with sales fluctuations in a firm's home market. If the markets in your domestic economy are in a down-cycle, exports may be able to pick up the slack in plant capacity, helping to maintain economies of scale and profitability. However, this presents a danger if tradition-bound domestic management views exports as just a useful buffer to accommodate fluctuations in domestic demand. Such a mentality implies backing away from supporting exports once the domestic economy rebounds and returns the factories to capacity, where production is then reserved for home market legacy accounts. From an export management perspective, this is a self-inflicted disaster. Export customers, like any clients, look for continuity of supply and service. If a firm is not seen as committed to its customers' long-term success, but is just toying with exports as a short-term convenience, it will fail. The firm's investment in generating offshore revenue streams will then be wasted and its reputation tarnished.

Though hard to predict, an often realized additional benefit of export marketing is management's exposure to technologies and developments in other countries that can be used back in the home market. For example, in the beverage industry, the now common plastic screw cap on paper cartons for juice and value-added dairy products was not developed in the US. It was a Japanese market innovation. Once understood, it was incorporated by processors to competitive advantage back in the US. Such openness to learning from other markets, and the rolling-out of the *Spout-Pak* domestically, directly benefited the US paper companies by further extending the paper carton's product life cycle.

## *Organizing for Exporting*

Manufacturers interested in serving overseas markets have fundamental decisions to make, including how to organize operations in both the home country and the overseas target market. Home country issues can involve deciding whether to work with an external firm that specializes in exporting to a geographic area or has expertise in handling a specific range of products, or whether the firm should look to assign and develop export responsibility in-house.

If a firm is small or chooses not to perform its own export marketing and promotion, there are export service providers that can help. These include ETCs (export trading companies), EMCs (export management companies), export merchants, export brokers, manufacturers' export representatives and export distributors. An EMC is often retained by several companies that lack export experience and acts as their collective export department. EMCs can perform a variety of services, including marketing research, channel selection, financing, shipping arrangements and documentation.

Most companies look to handle export operations in-house, and this should be the longer-term goal of any globally oriented firm. In a small firm, such responsibilities may sometimes be incorporated into an existing employee's domestic job description. An obvious advantage of this low-cost approach is that it requires no additional personnel. However, this can only work effectively if the domestic employee is thoroughly competent in terms of product and customer knowledge and if the export target market has customer characteristics similar to the familiar domestic market. One example (and not an especially good one) is a Canadian company shipping into New York or Kansas. In such a case, the requirement for specialized knowledge is reduced. However, the layering-on of export responsibility to Asian markets on such an employee, and for management to expect that person to understand and manage the vagaries of such a task would hardly be sensible, and any perceived savings would prove to be a classic false-economy.

Strategically-minded firms will determine that they need a dedicated and skilled staff to handle and grow exports. Export responsibilities can also be handled by separate divisions in a firm or within a specific export-oriented organizational structure. A company that assigns a sufficiently high priority to its export business will establish an in-house organization.

A critical step in export success is for a company to interview and then select a Foreign Freight Forwarder (we will just use the term 'Forwarder'). This is a highly specialized outside company that acts almost as an extension of your organization, and, over time, an almost organic relationship between the firm and its Forwarder will develop. Export traffic management and documentation are complex and a Forwarder handles this vital work on behalf of the firm and removes much of the stress of operating internationally. Forwarders, essentially, are retained to handle a firm's logistics and documentation needs. On behalf of a firm, the Forwarder handles relations with railroads, trucking and ocean carriers. They can arrange the inland move from factory to port of embarkation, book the freight with a shipping line, arrange for transfers, warehousing, shipment consolidation, customs clearance, ocean insurance, consularizations and certificates of origin. Forwarders can help assemble the documentary package associated with such terms of sale as documents-against-payment or letters of credit. Forwarders provide the same (but in reverse) services for importing firms. Whether to retain a Forwarder does not depend upon a company's size, as both small and large firms utilize their services, regardless of whether a company has a capable traffic department. Larger Fortune 500 firms may use several Forwarders, each working closely on the needs of a specific division.

## Representation & Distribution

With in-house export capability being developed, a firm also must decide how best to manage in-market sales representation and product distribution in the target market. A fundamental question is whether a firm should use direct market representation (using its own professional staff) or be represented by a third-party intermediary?

a) **Direct Representation**—The major advantages of direct representation in a market are control and communication. Direct representation means that decisions on market development, resource allocation, and pricing can be implemented unilaterally. Moreover, when a product is new-to-market, special efforts are necessary to induce trial and support follow-on sales. Direct representation helps ensure that these efforts are closely managed and will optimize the marketer's investment. The other great advantage of direct representation is that it provides immediate feedback from the market. Such feedback can vastly improve export marketing decisions on product, price, communications, and distribution, enabling improved tailoring of one's marketing offer.

Direct representation does not necessarily mean that the exporter sells directly to the end-user. Most global sales are in fact B2B and ultimately depend upon derived demand. Direct representation involves selling to wholesalers, retailers or manufacturers that incorporate the exporter's materials/components into their finished products. A disadvantage of direct representation is the cost of maintaining a capable sales and marketing staff in the overseas market or region. The ongoing costs of keeping such global staff in the field, compared to domestic sales, are significant. Such direct representatives may be local hires or 'road warriors' from the exporter's home country, or if the market potential is significant, an expatriate manager may permanently reside in-country. Such a person would be selected from the elite cadre of a firm's managers, with all their attendant high costs.

b) **Independent Representation**—In many markets, low sales volumes may not justify the cost of maintaining direct representation. This depends less upon the size of the country than upon the size of the specific market opportunity within that country or region. As significant sales volumes are required to justify the costs of direct representation, the use of an independent agency or distributor is often an effective means of accessing a market. In this case, finding a capable and trustworthy agent and/or distributor will be the key to export success.

Independent representatives or distributors (sometimes called value-added resellers) often handle a range of products for several companies, as there often is simply not enough volume or incentive for independents to invest in representing a single company or product line. Now, a word of caution. Marketers should perform careful due diligence on any prospective agent or representative, interview several, thoroughly check their local reputation and industry knowledge, and not rush to embrace any local company. In developing markets, a key criteria to assess is the level of personal friendships and connections that a local agent or representative has with local industry leaders and government officials. Much more than in the 'low-context' business environments of Europe and North America, business relations in developing markets or NICs (newly industrialized countries) are 'high-context' and business is often facilitated when relations between your agent and the key accounts evidence a longstanding personal rapport. Having a local agent represent your company is a natural and common evolutionary step in export development. Agents provide expertise in understanding the local industry, the cultural and legal environment, plus will have connections inside key government agencies that can assist with shipment documentation, local logistics and customs clearance. The local agent or representative keeps track of customer marketing needs, keeps an eye on client inventories and provides valuable market guidance and feedback to the exporter. While using agents is often the correct and necessary step in entering and growing a market, managers should nonetheless be very sure to understand the legal ramifications of entering into an agency agreement. If an agency turns out to be non-productive, or the market grows to where direct representation is justified and the agent is no longer needed, it can be difficult, time-consuming and costly to terminate the association. Local agents will likely benefit from local political support (the perception of a small local company fighting an exploitive MNC) as well as a legal system biased in favor of local citizens. This is a reality in both NICs and advanced trading nations, such as Israel or the Netherlands.

From a management perspective, the selected local agent should also not represent a firm's competitors. This should be obvious. However, an agent with *complementary* product lines to a firm's export offerings should be embraced as they can provide marketing synergies. For example, even though IP has a global presence and skilled international managers, the company chose to enter into agreements with local agents in the secondary Asian markets of Singapore, Malaysia and Thailand. These agents, in addition to promoting IP's packaging, also represented the manufacturers of sophisticated carton filling equipment that would 'form-fill-seal' the IP cartons. These complementary offerings provided an attractive single-source marking approach, one that was appreciated by dairy and beverage processors. A further point is that the fewer product lines that an agent represents, the less dilution of their efforts on a company's behalf. Agents are typically paid on a commission basis and this is their incentive to develop the local market for the exporter. From the exporter's perspective, the cost of such local representation is only borne if sales are achieved. The level of commission varies by agent and market. In many markets, agents are paid a 3% to 5% commission on the FOB value of regular shipments (and are paid once the exporter is paid).

*A side note*: FOB is shipping nomenclature for 'free on board,' meaning the value of a product delivered to the dock at the exporter's port of embarkation. Technically, this actually means put on board a vessel, but for practical purposes means delivery to the port of shipment. Under FOB terms, the inland move between the exporter's facility and the port is paid by the exporter. Another common term of sale is C&F. This is 'cost and freight' with the cost being the sales price of the product (equivalent to FOB) plus the cost of the ocean freight to a named port of delivery being factored into the C&F quote and the cost paid for by the exporter. Sales are also made under the term CIF. This is the same as C&F, but with the addition of ocean insurance to the named port of delivery being factored into the CIF quote and the cost paid for by the exporter. Now, back to compensating your local agent. It is reasonable to pay them on the FOB value, but not pay commissions on ocean freight or insurance.

If sales and shipments are infrequent (such as for machinery), compensation levels may move to the 12% to 15% level. The variance is because such sales are quite different. The logic is that some sales, such as milk carton sales, are *roll-over* business (i.e., ongoing, month after month) and require only routine 'care and feeding' by the agent after the basic supplier agreement has been established. This compares to a *one-off* sale of a specific piece of equipment, a sale that requires a great deal of effort and months to secure, and the kind of sale that might not recur for years. It bears noting that export managers factor the commissions and fees of their agents and Freight Forwarders (discussed above) into the company's export pricing.

A further point is that globally minded companies with long-term horizons may forecast (in fact plan) that a market's volume will expand to a level that justifies direct representation and/or actual in-country production. In expectation of such a development, managers may well enter into an agency agreement in anticipation that after a few years the exporting firm would absorb the agency as a logical step in expanding their firm's presence in an offshore market. There is inherent logic in this as the local agent will have already established a deep working relationship with the exporter, understand the exporter's product line, be well known to the trade, and have the cultural skills to assist and guide the forward-integration of the company locally. This is precisely the approach taken by IP. When market conditions were appropriate, IP's independent sales agents in both Taiwan and South Korea were brought inside the newly incorporated firms to take on important management roles.

Finally, the choice of whether to use an agent or a distributor for market entry depends upon the specific product and market; there is no firm rule. Agents add channel value in handling import/export sales with a limited number of customers (not more than a few dozen and often B2B). However, while agents assist with invoice collections, they do not take title to the goods and have no 'skin in the game.' Distributors, on the other hand, add channel value where there are hundreds (if not thousands) of customers, such as retail outlets. Distributors take title, add their margin, and resell to the trade. Using distributors provides additional value as exporters are paid directly by distributors and therefore the exporter doesn't have to chase end-user receivables in offshore markets.

## Distribution Case Study—[yellow tail] wines enter the US[2]

What started as a small family winery in the Australian 'outback' has become the leading imported wine in the US. The reasons for this success present an instructive study in 'going international.' Back in 1997, John Casella of Casella Wines in New South Wales, Australia, was looking for a way to enter the lucrative US wine market, a market already saturated with over 6,500 competing labels. Casella knew his company didn't have the staff, resources or scale to enter the American market directly. Finding a reputable distributor with a deep understanding of the US market was thus imperative. In the same year, William J. Deutsch & Sons, an experienced wine distributor based in White Plains, New York, was looking to add an Australian wine label to its portfolio. The distributor's principal, Bill Deutsch, approached the Australian Trade Commission for assistance in identifying prospective exporters. At the same time, Casella Wines was asking its own government for assistance, and the Australian Trade Commission made the important connection. As noted in the prior chapter, this was a wise use of trade promotion offices. Such offices are fielded by most countries and staffed by business development specialists and commercial attachés. Bill Deutsch and John Casella then agreed to meet at a trade show in San Francisco, and, as Bill Deutsch says, "It was a perfect match." The first export shipment of Casella wine arrived in 1999. However, there were immediate quality issues due to out-of-spec corks and W.J. Deutsch had trouble moving the stock. This poor performance could easily have ended the supplier/distributor relationship. However, in an important demonstration of support, Bill Deutsch agreed to work through the problems and continue the relationship. The reader should note here that, even in this age of e-commerce, long-term success in global business still depends upon personal trust and mutual commitment. After thinking through next steps and with marketing input from Bill Deutsch and Casella's Marketing Director, Casella Wines developed an easy-drinking wine and positioned it as an approachable social drink, with an image intended to resonate with America's affection for the iconic laid-back Australian culture. The new wine, now under the [yellow tail] label, was targeted to exploit the largely uncontested segment between low-end jug wines and premium wines.

The plan was that jug-wine drinkers could be induced to trade-up to the very drinkable wine, while premium wine drinkers would trade-down to the good quality but value-priced [yellow tail]. The strategy succeeded well beyond Casella Wines' or W.J. Deutsch's expectations; shipments grew from an initial trial of 60,000 cases in 2001 to over 8 million cases annually. Also, and in what has now become a template for other wine distributors, W.J. Deutsch negotiated a 50% ownership of the [yellow tail] label in the US market. This is reasonable from a distributor's perspective, as having taken the risk of supporting and building a market for a label, one needs to have assurance that the supplier will not 'shop' the business to another distributor sometime in the future. Such joint ownership helps to ensure that both parties remain committed to a long-term collaboration.

Beyond the design and brilliant execution of the marketing mix, the two companies also worked closely on their mutual terms of sale from market entry to the much larger volumes of today. Initial sales were '90 days B/L,' meaning that W.J. Deutsch would remit payment 90 days from the date stamped on the B/L (an Ocean Bill of Lading, a document that evidenced shipment from Australia). Casella trusted W.J. Deutsch to pay on time and no bank intermediary was required. Casella mailed the B/L and draft for payment directly to the importer and then W.J. Deutsch (actually a Forwarder acting on W.J. Deutsch's behalf) would take the B/L (which also represents title to the shipment) and present it to the ocean carrier and then receive the shipment. After 90 days from the B/L date, W.J. Deutsch would remit payment to Casella Wines.

Alternatively, the two parties could have agreed to operate under what is called 'documents against acceptance,' a form of documentary collection. Casella would then have routed the Ocean Bill of Lading and a 90-day time draft to a correspondent bank in the US. Upon receipt, the bank would have notified the W.J. Deutsch Company, which would sign and thus 'accept' the time draft, and thereby formally pledge the company to pay the draft in 90 days. Upon such acceptance, the bank would release the document package (and therefore title) to the importer. After 90 days, W.J. Deutsch would 'honor the draft' and remit payment to Casella Wines. If payment were due upon receipt (the terminology is 'at sight'), the draft would be a 'sight draft' and not a time draft, and the importer would sign and pay the draft before the bank would release the document package.

From a risk-management perspective, this is a non-letter-of-credit transaction, and an exporter runs the liability of non-payment by the importer. More common in international transactions (at least until commercial relations have become well established) is the use of a Letter of Credit which can remove the dual risks of non-performance and non-payment. However, a high level of personal trust existed between Casella and Deutsch, and both preferred to operate without the constraints and fees associated with such Letters of Credit.

The reader can here refer to later Chapter 3 on Trade Documentation and Getting Paid. This shows a typical L/C (Letter of Credit) transaction and how a B/A (Bankers' Acceptance) is created. This happens when the originating bank (the importer's bank that opened the original L/C in favor of the exporter) endorses or 'accepts' the exporter's time draft. Once a time draft is accepted, the importer's credit worthiness is replaced by the bank's own guarantee to pay the B/A (the former time draft) at its maturity date. Such B/As are readily discounted by major banks or sold into the secondary market for additional financial liquidity.

As noted, and far beyond expectations, the sales of [yellow tail] grew faster than planned, and this presented a severe strain on Casella Wines' ability to meet demand. A key issue in the success or failure of a product launch is consistency and continuity of supply. [yellow tail] was close to a market failure. There are numerous Harvard Case Studies on how growth and success can kill a company. Casella was in danger of 'losing the market' and needed to rapidly ramp-up production and its wine shipments. As with most start-ups, they were perennially short of cash and urgently needed more capital equipment and operating funds. Further, the cash-short Casella Wines was unable to secure sufficient bank credit lines to grow the business. On the other side of the Pacific, the W.J. Deutsch Company (not being a bank) was not in a position to provide the cash and its business model followed the industry norm of 90-day terms. In effect, Casella's limited cash was tied-up in its product transiting the Pacific and through the 90-day payment terms. To manage this challenge, W.J. Deutsch worked with a very capable bank and arranged for an unusual form of B/A, known as a Clean Banker's Acceptance. Unlike a standard B/A, a Clean B/A does not involve an L/C, but does require close coordination with the importer's bank and the exporter's bank. With this structure, Casella's 90-day drafts were promptly 'accepted' by W.J. Deutsch's US bank. The resultant Clean B/As (now carrying the full faith and credit of a bank) could then be immediately discounted by Casella Wines and the cash used to address the critical cash shortage back in Australia. Without this flexibility, the market growth of [yellow tail] would have stumbled. This also demonstrates that with every success there are problems and challenges. Here the financial system fulfilled its role in serving the needs of clients and enabling global trade. As the business became established and [yellow tail] grew to become the leading imported wine label in the US, the companies moved to operate on an open account basis.

*A side note:* Occasionally, a manager may hear the term *aval* in association with a European transaction. An aval is a third-party guarantee provided by an *avalizor* (often the importer's bank, and for a fee) on a draft or promissory note. As above, the exporter could route the document package and draft to a correspondent local bank. The bank would release the documents (and title to the shipment) upon the importer signing a draft or promissory note which would be *avalized* by the bank. An aval provides the exporter recourse against an importer's non-payment, and such a bank-guaranteed receivable can also be discounted.

# *Licensing*

Licensing is a contractual arrangement where one company (the licensor) provides technology, know-how, patents, and/or a successful brand to another company (the licensee) in exchange for a licensing fee and an ongoing royalty stream. Licensing can be an appealing form of global market entry. A company can use licensing agreements with a foreign firm to supplement its domestic bottom-line with almost no capital or marketing costs. Over the life of the license agreement, licensing can offer an attractive return on a firm's prior investment in R&D, patents and know-how, providing the licensee adheres to the contract.

Licensing may seem to offer low financial or market exposure, but there are risks. A disadvantage of licensing is that it limits the licensor's direct involvement with the overseas market and the ability to truly understand the final end-user's needs or desires. A license may also limit a firm's upside profits from prospective in-market expansion or overseas manufacturing. There also is the risk that while the license agreement is in force, the licensee will fully absorb the technology and know-how of the licensor, develop its own abilities, and become globally competitive. Additionally, the licensee may even evolve into a direct competitor of the licensor, not just in their country, but in the original licensor's own home market. A topical example of this is the recent US$1.5 billion sale and installation of advanced wind turbines in Texas. The provider is not a US company, but the Chinese firm Shenyang Power Group. The wind turbines do not utilize Chinese technology, but technology licensed to the Chinese firm by the General Electric Company. GE's action as a licensor, looking for short-term financial gain, enabled their Chinese competitor (GE also sells wind turbines) to install the largest wind farm in the US, GE's home market.[3] The implications are significant. This large project gives Shenyang Power Group sufficient specialized experience and scale to now compete anywhere in the world. No other global competitor can match such scale, and thus cost advantage. An additional competitive point is that the Texas installation received beneficial project financing from the Export-Import Bank of China (utilizing the overhang of US$ reserves from China's mammoth trade surplus with the US). This directly relates to the brief introduction earlier on 'new trade theory' where national governments (here the Chinese) play an active role in a nation's competitiveness by supporting and encouraging nascent technologies/industries, providing the basis for scale and first-mover advantage.

Overall, managers should be careful that their licensing strategy ensures an ongoing competitive advantage. License arrangements can create further export market opportunities and open the door to low-risk manufacturing relationships. They also can speed diffusion of new products and technologies. When managers do decide to license, they should consider an agreement that anticipates more extensive market participation in the future, including ultimately entering into a future joint venture with the licensee.

## *Franchising*

Franchises are a variation on licensing and fall into several categories. These include manufacturer-sponsored franchises (such as a Ford or Honda independent car dealership) and service-firm-sponsored retail franchises (such as Jiffy Lube or Pizza Hut). Franchises are now a major part of the US economy; some calculate they are as much as half of domestic US retail sales.[4] For this discussion, we will focus on the remarkable global growth of service-firm franchises like McDonald's and KFC. Franchising is a contractual arrangement where a company, the franchisor, sells the rights to its brand, logo and business model to a franchisee to establish a new company (perhaps a SUBWAY restaurant) in a specific location or region. Typically, the franchisor receives an ongoing fee (a specific percentage of the franchisee's revenues). The fees or royalties go toward ongoing operational support, R&D, marketing programs, and profit back to the franchisor. A franchise fee is commonly limited in time and expires at the end of a specific term (though the franchisee and franchisor may elect to renew the contract). If there is a breach of trust, then the contract expires. In some markets, McDonald's will actually own the land/buildings and lease them back to franchisees for the life of the agreement. In this case, they have strong leverage on the franchisee and can step in and refranchise the restaurant if there are problems. Franchising has proven to be a remarkably successful business model. Both parties, the franchisee and the franchisor, have a mutual interest in the franchise's success. The franchisor's business model (such as Pizza Hut's) and management processes are proven. The franchisor's logo and brand identity (such as McDonald's) are well known. Franchisees typically are local entrepreneurs who have placed their own investment capital at risk (have 'skin in the game') and so will work far harder than hourly employees to ensure success. Also, being local, the franchisee will have a better understanding of an area's market and regulations (such as zoning) and be better positioned for governmental approvals than some distant corporate entity. The franchisee receives support via the transfer of business process know-how, plus staff and management training. By being part of a proven association, the franchisee also has greater access to bank loans and credit lines than other start-up companies because bankers know that most non-affiliated small businesses fail. Finally, a franchise system with hundreds of franchisees benefits from far greater economies of scale in procurement, logistics, and advertising than a stand-alone firm.

The international growth of franchises has been one of the hallmarks of globalization. SUBWAY began as a small deli operation in Connecticut and began selling franchises in 1974. Today, there are over 33,000 SUBWAY restaurants globally, 30% outside the US and spread across 90 countries. Combining a well proven and continually refined business model with effective marketing and local entrepreneurial ownership drives this success. The author recalls an evening stroll in the old souk (market) in the Saudi Arabian capital of Riyadh, turning a corner and coming face to face with a SUBWAY restaurant doing a lively business. The place was staffed by well-trained imported Philippine workers serving patrons of a dozen nationalities. If ever global trade created a confluence of diverse cultures, this certainly was one such place.

## Franchise Case Study—KFC enters China[5]

When China reengaged with the world in the 1980s, its economy grew at unprecedented double-digit rates driven by export trade enabled by abundant inexpensive labor. As the Chinese economy matured, more value-added products were produced, providing greater profits to China's growing cadre of entrepreneurs. The global demand for Chinese products increased exporter margins and ultimately workers' wages. Though under reported in the West, China's coastal cities have faced a tightening supply of qualified workers, labor rates have risen and a nascent middle class is developing. As the wages of labor increased, so too did the ability of workers to afford 'international-quality' consumer goods. Perhaps due in part to past hardships, there is a societal recognition that when Chinese have disposable income, one of their immediate lifestyle changes is to move 'up-market' in food consumption. The diet in urban centers is changing from grains and vegetables to a greater emphasis on the consumption of pork and poultry.

The management of KFC recognized this evolving market opportunity, and established the first fast-food restaurant in China in 1987. KFC's sister brand Pizza Hut followed in 1990. In 1992, KFC introduced the entrepreneurial concept of franchising to China. The success of this market and consumer-driven business model has been spectacular. Today, there are thousands of KFC restaurants in 550 cities across China, with a new restaurant opening nearly every day. KFC is part of a family of franchise brands operated by Louisville-based Yum! Brands. These include Pizza Hut, Taco Bell, Long John Silver and A&W. Globally, 80% of the Yum-branded stores are owned by independent franchise operators. During the initial years of the China launch, KFC went to market with a mix of both traditional franchises and company-owned restaurants. Today, the majority of KFC restaurants in China are company-owned. The rationale is that China's infrastructure is not well developed and direct management helps ensure both marketing and quality control during the key market-entry phase. This control also rapidly drove the food service category in China and so secured for KFC the benefits of being first-to-market. Geographic expansion was based upon saturating markets in sequence, with an initial focus on 1st tier cities, then 2nd tier cities, then 3rd tier, etc. Regional KFC managers were encouraged to localize menus and focus on food innovation, all part of tailoring offerings to local needs, yet all under the umbrella and cachet of a global brand. As YUM! Brands Senior Vice President Joaquin Pelaez commented, "The Chinese consumer loves western brands because they trust western brands. KFC is the most recognizable brand in China . . . a foreign brand with a Chinese heart."[6] Both KFC and Pizza Hut had first-mover advantage, not only with selling into largely uncontested markets, but also tactically, as they rapidly secured high-traffic real estate to position themselves for the anticipated rise in consumer affluence. This early decision to own the best retail locations has preempted competitor expansion. McDonald's entered China three years behind KFC. They were not as aggressive in entering the market and today have only a third of YUM! Brand's market presence. KFC's success vis-à-vis McDonald's also has cultural roots. The Chinese diet has traditionally included poultry (including, yes, the famous Peking Duck), so a menu based on chicken is an easy step. In contrast, ground-up meat patties have not been a traditional part of the Chinese diet, so building an appreciation for western-style beef burgers requires a longer time-line.

Once a KFC restaurant opened, local consumers immediately appreciated the friendly and non-bureaucratic customer service (an important perceived attribute). Internally, management built a culture around the term, "Yum Customer Mania." A further point of distinction is KFC's very visible and well promoted focus on food safety (something often taken for granted in the West, but not in China). KFC's China management is truly local (nearly no expats), yet the international branding, staff training and quality control are world class and continue to generate strong customer preference. By 2010, China was generating US$4 billion in sales and had become the principal source of operating profits within the global YUM system of 37,000 restaurants in over 100 countries.

## *Investment—Joint Venture and Foreign Direct Investment*

After companies gain experience outside their home country through exporting, licensing or an in-country distributor, the time comes when managers may well look for a deeper level of participation in an offshore market. A JV (joint venture) with a local partner represents a far more extensive form of participation in a foreign market than either exporting or licensing. A JV is a collaboration between two or more firms on a specific project to serve one or more markets. This often takes the form of an equity investment (sometimes also called an equity-joint-venture or, simply, an EJV) between two companies in the creation of a third company. The 'parent' companies remain independent but commit resources to support the new entity. The advantages of this strategy include the sharing of risk and the ability to combine different, hopefully complementary, strengths, i.e., a blending of marketing with manufacturing expertise. One JV partner might have in-depth knowledge of a local market, an extensive distribution system, or access to low-cost labor or raw materials. The other partner might be a foreign firm with a global brand, product expertise, process knowledge or technology. Firms with limited capital resources might seek partners to jointly finance projects. Also, a JV may be the only way to enter a country if the government awards business routinely to local companies or if there are laws that prohibit foreign-controlled firms but do allow JVs. Proceeding with either a JV or a 'wholly-owned' enterprise, the new company can accrue market advantages through closer relations with customers, as well as providing improved customer service and technical support. The company also can serve customers with much shorter order and delivery lead-times via local production, as compared to conventional ocean shipments.

In each market, the decision whether to position oneself in a JV or as a wholly-owned enterprise must be decided on each specific market's merits. Managers must be clear on what each partner brings to the table. Also, managers need to ascertain what are the interests and capabilities of their prospective partners going forward. JVs can be hard to sustain because partners may have different capabilities, resources and objectives. Cross-cultural differences in managerial styles also present challenges. This is an issue not only in the Americas or Asia, but can also be seen in the clash of corporate cultures of Germany's Daimler-Benz and America's Chrysler which contributed significantly to that venture's failure.

As noted, each decision is market-specific. For example, the government of the PRC, the People's Republic of China, often favors joint-ventures over a WFOE (a Wholly Foreign Owned Enterprise). JVs facilitate the transfer of foreign technologies, know-how and modern business processes. A further push toward the joint-venture model in China is that a WFOE may lack the necessary trade and governmental connections (known as guān-xì, pronounced: *gwang-she*) to succeed.

Just across the Straits of Formosa from the PRC is the ROC (Republic of China/Taiwan), a market economy and one of the economic tigers of Asia. Global firms have greater latitude there in the form of investment, and both JVs and wholly-owned subsidiaries of foreign firms are welcome.

In a JV, partners share the profits, risks and control, and an investor should not underestimate the significant management time required to handle the many issues associated with working with a JV partner. Given that control is shared, success will depend upon the caliber of executive leadership of the new enterprise. Only the best global managers should be tasked with such postings. While management of a majority-owned or wholly-owned enterprise will face many issues, they will not face the ongoing, and at times contentious, issues of control, authority, and strategic direction as they would in a JV partnership. Companies with wholly-owned affiliates/subsidiaries have full control over operations, marketing, financial strategies, structure, human resources, etc.

## Joint Venture Case Study—Tropicana enters Japan[7]

Today, the sixty-year-old *Tropicana* brand accounts for two-thirds of not-from-concentrate juice sales in the US. In addition to its domestic position, it is also a familiar brand internationally; *Tropicana's* first not-from-concentrate exports went to France in 1966. However, it was not until 1991 that *Tropicana* found a way to enter Japan, one of the world's largest and most affluent economies, yet also one of the most difficult markets to access. One of the numerous market hurdles is that Japan, unlike North America and Europe, requires packaged juices to carry a 14-day date-code for its shelf life. This rule was based upon the historic practice of date-coding milk after World War II. However, juice is a low pH product, and pathogenic bacteria that survive in milk simply are not viable in juice. With good quality control, freshly pasteurized (flash heated and cooled) juice actually has a shelf life of more than two months. Ocean shipping times between the US and Japan simply couldn't accommodate the 14-day production-to-sales window. So, to sell in Japan, *Tropicana* management recognized that it had to address four key in-market issues:

1. Bulk chilled and frozen juice would need to be imported and locally processed, packaged and date-coded.
2. In-country distribution would need to be secured.
3. Ongoing quality control (QC) would need to be assured on both sides of the Pacific.
4. Culturally sensitive marketing and brand-management would need to be established.

A frequent approach by global companies to the Japanese market is to collaborate with an established local firm. In fact, trying to set up an independent operation in Japan is culturally problematic and would require years to achieve (if at all). Additionally, product distribution in Japan is an arcane, multi-tiered process based on company and personal relationships that go back decades. From a real-world perspective, firms entering Japan should not delude themselves that they have any ability to self-distribute.

In 1988, ten years before its acquisition by PepsiCo, *Tropicana* was part of the Seagram Company, then the largest distiller of alcoholic beverages in the world. Seagram already had a JV with the Japanese brewer Kirin, a marketer of premium brands of alcohol and spirits. Seagram's management judged that the JV relationship (Kirin-Seagram) could be levered to introduce the premium juice brand *Tropicana* into Japan. To proceed and also manage the many market access issues, a new JV was formed between *Tropicana* (a division of Seagram) and Kirin Beverage Corporation (the soft drink arm of the Kirin conglomerate). As noted above, a JV should be synergistic and combine the capabilities of the various partners, capabilities that are complementary and that neither can provide separately. *Tropicana* had a globally recognized product, brand-management, marketing know-how, and expertise in process and quality control. Kirin had capable in-country staff, proven distribution channels, and longstanding trade and operational contacts throughout Japan. The logic was that the collective abilities of the partners could build a formidable market presence in the premium juice segment. The JV is a 50-50 partnership, with all marketing, advertising, and operational costs shared equally; profits are shared via a complex transfer pricing mechanism. Chilled bulk juice is imported by the logistics arm of Kirin Beverage. These bulk shipments are then delivered to dairy and beverage plants across Japan for processing and packaging. The plants are 'contract-packers' (often processors with excess capacity) with whom the Kirin production arm contracts to process and package the juice. Contract-packers are paid for this service, but do not take title to the product. *Tropicana* assures QC of all the citrus juices and shares its proprietary process technology for its *Pure Premium* branded juice. Juice can be processed and cartons formed/filled/sealed on the same stainless steel equipment as milk, so the JV benefited from such in-place 'swing capacity' at Japan's dairies. The juice for the JV's market launch was first processed under contract by the Koiwai Dairy Company, a plant partially owned by Kirin.

Such contract-packing arrangements are mutually beneficial. *Tropicana* and the JV avoided the need to make a major capital investment in a greenfield operation. They did not have to deal with local approvals, construction delays or labor hiring and training issues. So, without operational delays, *Tropicana Pure Premium* juice was able to get to market promptly after the Kirin-Tropicana JV was established. After contract-packing, the retail juice is sold at an agreed-upon-transfer price by the JV to Kirin Beverage (the JV's only customer). Kirin Beverage then adds its distributor mark-up as it sells the finished product into the trade.

Marketing managers appreciate the value of speed-to-market, and the prospect for such a key competitive benefit should always be pursued. A nimble firm with first-mover advantage can establish a market presence that rapidly provides associated cost advantages of scale economies. Follow-on competitors often face extended periods before reaching profitable scale.

The contract-packers also benefit from the arrangement, as the additional through-put enables them to better cover the heavy fixed capital costs of their productive assets (the reader should recall the first chapter's discussion of 'over and under absorbed burden' in tracking and managing costs).

Up to this point, *Tropicana* had addressed three of the four critical issues for success in Japan. And while going to market in Japan with a major player like Kirin was foundational, ultimate success would depend upon the competence of the JV's senior management. This is a central point and one of the underlying themes for global managers to focus on. As noted, a JV presents major management challenges, particularly so in Japan where one must understand and navigate a complex and often opaque business culture. The Tropicana-Kirin JV not only needed a bi-lingual manager, but one who could understand both Japanese and American world views. Acting as a bridge between two diverse corporate cultures, the manager would need to keep all sides focused and collaborating in the right direction. At the same time, the manager would be responsible for quality brand-management, product development and consumer education. After a professional search, the necessary high-caliber manager was identified and hired. Of interest is that the JV manager was not only bi-lingual and bi-cultural, but also a US citizen and the fourth generation of his family to reside in Japan. His great-grandfather traveled to Japan as a language teacher from Harvard in the late 19th century.

With the four key commercial factors in place, the first cartons of *Tropicana* from concentrate juice entered the market under the Kirin-Tropicana company name in 1991. *Tropicana Pure Premium* followed in 1992. The *Tropicana* rollout was a success, and the brand with its 'American cachet' (brilliantly reinforced at times with such iconic music as *"in the summertime when the weather is fine . . ."* by the band Mungo Jerry) continues to hold a leading share in one of the world's most competitive and quality-conscious markets.

## Ownership & Investment

The desire for control and ownership of operations outside of a firm's home country drives the decision to make an FDI (Foreign Direct Investment). This can either be a greenfield investment or the acquisition of plant, equipment, or other assets outside the home country. By definition, direct investment presumes that the investor has control or significant influence over the investment. This compares to a portfolio investment where the investor has a passive role without significant influence or management control. An operational definition of direct investment is ownership of at least 20 percent of the equity of a company.

The most extensive form of participation in global markets is 100 percent ownership of a foreign subsidiary, which may be achieved by a start-up or acquisition. Such ownership requires a significant commitment of capital and managerial effort, but offers the fullest level of market participation. Companies here move beyond accessing a market via exports and a local agent to direct investment and ownership to achieve faster expansion, greater control, and higher profits. However, acquisitions are fraught with hidden danger, and significant due diligence should be pursued. In the People's Republic of China there are great risks in pursuing equity deals. Local firms are known to falsify their balance sheets for tax and other reasons, and overseas managers face minefields of off-balance sheet liabilities, verbal barter agreements and commitments associated with governmental favors and guān-xì. It also is not uncommon to have signage changed on a facility the day before a foreign partner arrives for a tour or a signing ceremony.[8] Beyond equity deals, even the straight purchase of assets can be problematic. A foreign firm will need to have a registered legal entity that is allowed to accept the assets, and in some cases, assets are simply not transferrable under local law. The benefit of an acquisition is that it can be a relatively prompt and sometimes less expensive approach to market entry than starting a greenfield business. It also may have the added advantage of avoiding communication and conflict-of-interest problems that can arise with the JV model. Nonetheless, acquisitions still present the challenging task of integrating the acquired company into a firm's worldwide organization.

Several of the advantages of the JV model also apply to wholly-owned subsidiaries, including access to markets and avoidance of tariff or quota barriers. Like JVs, ownership enables the transfer of new technology, experience and manufacturing know-how to a new national market. The wholly-owned investment model also accrues the control and profits of full ownership. All such investments require a major commitment of managerial time and energy. The decision to invest abroad, whether by expansion or acquisition, also can clash with a domestic firm's short-term profitability goals and present significant financial exposure to the parent company. At times, this may become a contentious issue for publicly-held companies where significant shareholder home-country assets are put at risk when invested in a foreign regulatory environment. Despite these challenges, global trade and investment continue to present great opportunities, so the establishment of FDIs continues.

## Foreign Direct Investment Case Study—International Paper Company in Asia

In the 1980s, International Paper Company made the market decision to forward-integrate into Japan and the Tigers of Asia. IP already was serving these markets on an export basis from plants in the US, but now looked to expand its B2B volumes and competitive position *inside* these increasingly affluent markets.

As the first step in this sequence, IP established a majority-owned company in Japan, a market of 127 million people. As noted earlier, foundational to the success of a foreign company in Japan is collaboration with a strong local partner. IP joined with the Ishizuka Glass Company to form a new company called IPI. Just as IP in the US was losing market share to a substitute form of packaging, so too was Ishizuka Glass in Japan. The dairy market in Japan was transitioning away from glass bottles (for over a century the traditional package for milk) to paper. Ishizuka Glass recognized the logic of protecting its eroding market position in the dairy sector by extending its product line with popular paper cartons. A sensible and timely way to do this was via a partnership with IP, the leading global producer of paperboard and consumer packaging. Consistent with the previously noted Tropicana experience in Japan, IP's local partner enabled the venture to get to market as it held 'approved vendor' status with processors—something developed over time and through close personal relationships (sometimes spanning generations). So strong were these entrenched channels that even though the US majority-owned venture IPI would produce the milk and juice cartons, IPI would first sell the cartons to Ishizuka Glass, which would then on-sell the cartons into the trade; Ishizuka was the recognized and approved vendor of record, not IPI.

Second in the market development sequence after Japan was South Korea (with 48 million people), a market with somewhat more transparent distribution channels. While governmental approvals were delayed by a protectionist bureaucracy and 'non-scientific' governmental considerations, ultimately the venture named International Paper Korea (IPK) did proceed. With high-quality in-market production and technical support, IPK built a dominant market position. Recalling our earlier comments on market entry and agents, IPK was incorporated with the local sales agency firm taking a minority equity position with the very capable director of the agency subsequently selected as president of the new firm.

Third in sequence for in-country production was Taiwan, a market of 23 million people (a population size similar to that of Australia). This was developed as a classic FDI. The market was initially served on an export basis from IP's West Coast plants. Under the strategic plan, exports would continue until the market achieved the critical mass necessary to justify an investment in the local manufacture of packaging. As the market grew, and per plan, a wholly-owned company was incorporated and a greenfield converting plant was built. During the volume ramp-up, IP's US-based marketing staff worked in-country with a local Taiwanese agent. And, again in line with plan, once the factory was built and the wholly-owned International Paper-Taiwan (IPT) incorporated, the local agency was absorbed into IPT as its in-house sales staff.

IPT benefited from significant first-mover advantage and took a dominant share. There were no other liquid packaging plants in Taiwan, and competitors from the US and Europe had to operate on an import-basis. Imported carton shipments had a time-line from order-entry through ocean shipment and ultimate customs clearance of six to eight weeks. Naturally, a dairy manager can never allow a plant to run out of packaging (that's a lot of milk on the floor), so the dairies' working-capital investment in packaging inventory had to cover several months of production packaging as a reserve. In contrast, IPT provided local *just-in-time* delivery, so the processing plants could hold minimal inventories (at a major reduction to their working capital cost). Such short lead-times provided a further marketing benefit. New products are frequently launched by dairy and juice processors, and if their market success yields better than expected sales, additional packaging could be promptly produced and delivered. The processor would then not fail to meet demand, lose the market, or alienate stores and supermarkets (being out of stock when the consumer is trying to give you money is a cardinal sin in retail). Long lead-time imports could not provide this quick response or flexibility to such derived demand. A further benefit to IPT was that its market pricing was enhanced by a significant *duty-umbrella*, also known as a *duty-cover*. Like many countries,

Taiwan looks to secure the benefits of employment and technology transfer that come from foreign investment and value-added production. Taiwan therefore established relatively low import duty levels to encourage the import of raw materials (to which value could be added) in tandem with relatively high import duties on value-added finished goods. IPT would import basic roll-stock from IP's primary mills in the US, and these entered Taiwan with a low tariff burden. Competitive carton imports, as finished goods, entered Taiwan subject to a relatively high tariff. This then set a relatively high, import-driven, market price for beverage cartons for the local juice and dairy processors. Under this tariff-induced market price umbrella, IPT established healthy in-market pricing and generated a significant financial return.

As to the other Economic Tigers of Hong Kong and Singapore, which have much smaller populations, they were served by a combination of exports from IPK, IPT and IP's West Coast plants.

## *Global Strategic Partnerships*

Finally, we briefly look at the business model known as a Global Strategic Partnership. This is a cooperative ventures between well-established global companies.

A GSP is not a merger but a form of JV where the parent companies remain independent after forming an alliance. The partners equally share both benefits and control and agree to make ongoing contributions to the partnership. The rationale for global companies forming a GSP can be driven by the need to share high development costs and know-how and/ or to provide new or collaborative access to markets. A GSP enables the partners to achieve something they could not achieve on a stand-alone basis.

## Global Strategic Partnership Case Study—Unilever and Pepsico

An example of a GSP between well managed global companies is the JV between the Anglo-Dutch Unilever and the US PepsiCo. They created an entity, Pepsi Lipton International (PLI), to cover the marketing and distribution of *Lipton* ready-to-drink (RTD) tea in select international markets.

As is typical with a GSP, the partners share ownership (50-50) and combine their separate strengths into something with great market logic. Unilever had the global *Lipton* brand, world-class product knowledge and ongoing tea R&D, but lacked both the go-to-market infrastructure and the know-how to compete effectively in the RTD beverage market. PepsiCo, a global food and beverage company, had an extensive bottling network, a skilled marketing staff and unparalleled distribution infrastructure, yet lacked an established tea brand to complement its product portfolio. PepsiCo also was looking to realign its revenues with a greater presence in the non-carbonated 'healthy' drink segment and away from the flat and declining carbonated beverage segment. The GSP enabled Unilever and PepsiCo to build market success that neither could have achieved separately. A closing note on the GSP: any venture that is a 50-50 construct requires highly competent management (recall the earlier discussion on the 50-50 Kirin-Tropicana JV). The terms of the GSP must be very carefully designed and negotiated, a complex process that can take well over a year. If there is to be long-term success, only the most capable global managers should be assigned to manage the alignment of such global organizations.

## *Some Closing Thoughts*

At the beginning of this short text, we devised the scenario where you, the reader, are a manager newly tasked with devising and executing a plan to expand offshore revenues. As a global manager, you must choose from a range of alternatives on how best to participate in offshore markets. Should this be via exporting, distribution, licensing, JV, FDI, or GSP? Each represents advantages and disadvantages. The choice will depend in part upon your firm's vision, expertise, and business model. Exporting can help a company build volume and achieve scale economies. Close cooperation with an overseas distributor can provide market access and offshore market feed-back. Licensing is a strategy to increase revenues with minimal investment and can be a good choice for a company with advanced technology or a strong brand image. Franchises can take a proven domestic business model overseas with rapid global penetration. JVs offer companies the opportunity to share risk and combine core competencies, but also require a long-term management commitment and careful planning and communication between the venture partners. Direct ownership, through a start-up or acquisition, similarly requires a major commitment of resources, both capital and managerial.

The preferred expansion strategy will depend upon your company's stage of development. Your firm may wish to use exporting and licensing to exploit headquarters' knowledge through a worldwide diffusion of products. Larger multinational companies can respond to local opportunities via acquisitions and greenfield manufacturing start-ups. Globally diversified companies can export products around the world from global-scale plants and benefit from a wealth of diverse intellectual capital.

This chapter has provided an overview of various avenues to successfully enter international markets, from initial exports to a full FDI. Successful exporting requires organizational decisions (including understanding internal and external levels of expertise), both in the home country and the target market. Skilled managers research how logistics and tariffs affect market opportunities. They also understand the mechanisms of international trade finance (see the next chapter). Finally, we again note that for cultural understanding and long term success, experienced marketers make a point of visiting potential markets before entering into substantive export or investment programs. Nothing compares to what can be learned on the ground, in-country.

[1]    J. Nocera, "China Tries to Solve Its Brand X Blues," *The New York Times*, 4/12/08.

[2]    The author is grateful for the generous assistance of Bill Deutsch, Chairman of W.J. Deutsch & Sons.

[3]    R. Smith, "Chinese-Made Turbines Will Fill Texas Wind Farm," *The Wall Street Journal*, 10/30/09.

[4]    See "Quick Franchise, Franchising, Facts and Statistics," accessed online at 'www.azfranchises.com,' 2012.

[5]    The author is grateful for the generous assistance of Albert Baladi, Managing Director of YUM Brands-Oceana.

[6]    J. Pelaez address to the Alltech Symposium, May, 2010.

[7]    The author is grateful for the generous assistance of Paul Guilfoile, Managing Director of Kirin-Tropicana.

[8]    J. Boyle and M. Winter, "A Different Toolbox for M&A Due Diligence in China," *Thunderbird International Business Review*, Vol. 51, February 2010.

# Chapter 3

## Trade Documentation and Getting Paid

While marketers need to understand the unique character of each international market and develop effective marketing plans to sell and serve that market, they also need to ensure that their terms of sale are competitive and that payments are received. The importance of getting paid for one's product or service should be obvious, but many managers new to international trade consider this only as an afterthought. One should never minimize the impact of not receiving timely payment on a significant sale to one's company, its employees, banking relationships and stakeholders. The consequences can be dire and put the viability of the company (and the marketer's career) at risk. As a manager, you need to appreciate the details at a granular level.

Experienced international managers consider the financial and shipping terms of a transaction as a normal part of negotiation with clients. When launching into international business, managers should already have an understanding of the specialized vocabulary and instruments of trade finance and documentation. This knowledge will be important to the manager's credibility and ability to work globally.

For our purposes, we will use the example of an imaginary export of, say, Modern Milking Equipment from an American exporter to a Farmers Cooperative in rural Turkey.

Compared to domestic transactions, international trade carries more complexity and risk. The importer and exporter (buyer and seller) often have little knowledge of each other. They also have limited ability to judge each other's credit risk or even a basic understanding of the other's legal and political environment. What if one company sends payment and the other fails to ship the product? Similarly, what if one company goes to the time and expense of producing and shipping the product, but the importer does not or cannot pay? Understandably, both importer and exporter are reluctant to put their companies at risk.

Trade can be entered into with different levels of risk, from the exporter accepting full or no transaction risk to the importer absorbing full or no transaction risk ('exposure'). If there is an established relationship between the two companies, the exporter may agree to operate on an "Open Account" basis. In this case, the Turkish importer orders a product; the American exporter produces and ships it and then invoices the customer for the sale. Upon the product's arrival, our Turkish importer simply wire-transfers payment to the American exporter.

In this scenario, the exporter takes on the full risk of non-payment by the customer. Open Account is commonly used domestically, but is rarely appropriate internationally, especially when the importer and exporter have little knowledge of each other. For the American exporter to have no risk, it may require prepayment known as "Cash in Advance" or "Cash with Order." Here the American exporter receives an upfront payment, and the Turkish importer bears the full financial risk should the exporter not ship as promised. If the Turkish importer has had limited dealings with the exporter, the importer is unlikely to accept such a risk. Also, like most purchasing managers in the US, the Turkish importer is likely to seek credit terms beyond the receipt of the goods or services. As an edge over a global competitor (such as a Swedish producer of Milking Equipment), our American exporter may need to provide extended payment terms.

In most transactions, neither party will wish to absorb the risks of non-performance by the exporter or non-payment by the importer. So how can this be resolved so that beneficial trade can proceed? Here the commercial parties can look to the international banking system. Acting in an intermediary role, international banks can remove the transaction risk from both the exporter and importer. Banks can, for a fee, provide assurance to the Turkish importer that the American exporter will perform as required and, concurrently, that the American exporter will receive payment for its products. In removing financial risk from the transaction, the banking system increases the volume and efficiency of international trade to the advantage of both the US and Turkey.

Managing risk is a key attribute of international banks and the "Letter of Credit" is a standard financial instrument used to achieve this. It is commonly referred to as an "L/C." It is important to note that the banking system works with and makes payments against documents, not contracts or relationships between companies; thus, the L/C is also known as a "documentary credit." Here, the exporter is assured of payment so long as it meets all the terms listed in the L/C that was "opened" in its favor, and the importer is not obligated to pay until the exporter has shipped the desired products.

*A word of caution*: Marketers have a responsibility to protect the interests of their company and should not allow themselves to be pressured away from requiring L/Cs for payment. This is good business practice and does not demonstrate a lack of trust or cultural bias against a prospective customer. Working out the terms of the L/C should be seen as a regular part of a commercial sale. Furthermore, if the local bank of the importer is reluctant to open an L/C in favor of the exporter (under the process outlined below), this may reflect either on the financial health of the importer or the soundness of the importer's bank, or even on possible constraints on that country's foreign exchange. Such reluctance by the importer's local bank should signal the exporter to be especially diligent with this transaction.

Other than in the most advanced economies, international marketers recognize that there is no effective legal recourse should a problem develop with an overseas customer. The L/C and the banking system can remove such exposure. In removing the risks of non-performance and non-payment, the international banking system significantly promotes the expansion of global trade. In our imaginary case, both our American exporter and Turkish importer have international trade experience and understand that discussing and finalizing the terms of an L/C is actually a very useful discipline, one that will minimize future misunderstandings or conflicts.

Our imaginary exporter and importer have worked out these commercial terms for their transaction:

- The American exporter will ship a specific set of Milking Equipment priced at US$5 million.
- The sale will be priced CIF Istanbul. This means that in addition to the price of the equipment, the American exporter (or its Freight Forwarder) will arrange for product delivery from its US factory to the port of Istanbul and has included in its price the cost of ocean freight and insurance for the shipment.
- The American exporter will send the equipment in one shipment within two months of the L/C being opened in its favor and be paid in US dollars.

- The exporter will accept payment six months after the Milking Equipment ships from a US port.
- The Turkish importer agrees to arrange for an Irrevocable L/C and pay local Turkish bank fees.
- Both parties will advise each other of the banks with which each will work in this transaction.

*A side note*: In a standard CIF quote, the *importer,* not the exporter, is responsible for the costs of local delivery from its domestic port, including local duties and fees. In most cases, L/Cs are "*irrevocable,*" meaning that the importer cannot subsequently revoke the L/C created in favor of the exporter. In reality, Revocable L/Cs are rarely used. In our transaction, the L/C document will note that it is "*irrevocable.*"

The L/C will specify what is to be shipped, when and to where shipment is to be made, the associated documents required, terms of sale: Ex Works, FOB (Free on Board), CIF (Cost Insurance Freight), etc.), the currency of payment ($, €, ¥, etc.), credit terms, the form of L/C (Irrevocable, Revocable, Stand-By) and who will pay the L/C and bank fees.

Now, let us look at how the commercial terms above are converted into a documentary credit (the L/C), a process that has greatly enabled international commerce through the years. There are four general steps:

**Step 1.** The Turkish importer asks its local Turkish bank to "open" a US$5 million Irrevocable Letter of Credit "in favor" of the American exporter (known now as the L/C's "beneficiary"). The L/C is payable upon the American exporter meeting the L/C documentary requirements. If the Turkish importer has good financial standing, the Turkish bank opens the L/C.

*Key point*: The Turkish importer's credit has now been replaced by the credit of the Turkish bank; the exporter relies on the bank's promise of payment, not the importer's.

To ensure that the American exporter performs as agreed, the importer will stipulate that the credit only be payable upon presentation of a set of documents agreed to by both exporter and importer. Again, this is why it is called a documentary credit. A basic list of documents noted in an L/C can include:

- Signed Commercial Invoices (reflecting the price and product)
- Time Drafts (instructing the importer to pay an amount at a future date)

- Full set of Ocean Bills of Lading
- Packing List
- Insurance Certificate
- Certificate of Origin (provided by the Chamber of Commerce)

These documents will evidence shipment of the Milking Equipment from the Port of Baltimore. The L/C will also state that partial shipments are not allowed and that payment in US dollars is to be made 180 days from date of the Bill of Lading, commonly referred to as a "B/L." This is a very specialized document that can serve as a receipt for the goods, a contract to transport the goods, and the actual title to the goods. A B/L is date-stamped when the common carrier accepts the export cargo for shipment. Also, like many companies, our American exporter uses the services of a specialized company known as a Freight Forwarder. Such companies arrange the logistics and insurance for shipments and help prepare the document package required under the L/C.

In our example, the American exporter can expect payment 180 days from the B/L date. The Turkish importer will not receive title (the Bill of Lading) to the shipment until either payment to the Turkish bank has been made or future payment (after 180 days from B/L date in our transaction) has been assured. Note: If immediate payment had been agreed upon, the terms in the L/C would have said payable "at sight," and "Drafts" would be listed in the document package not "Time Drafts." When Drafts and the other documents are presented to the importer's bank, the credit in favor of the American exporter would be honored immediately "at sight."

**Step 2.** The Turkish bank, known as the "Issuing bank" or "Opening bank," then advises the American exporter's bank that the above L/C has been opened in favor of the exporter. The American bank, now known as the "Advising bank" or the "Negotiating bank," advises the American exporter that the credit is in place.

**Step 3.** The American exporter carefully reviews the terms in the L/C to ensure that they match those previously agreed to (even misspellings can be a problem). Should corrections be needed, an Amended L/C will need to be generated by the Issuing Bank. If the exporter believes it can meet the terms of the L/C, it will proceed to produce and ship the Modern Milking Equipment.

**Step 4.** Once the Milking Equipment ships from the Port of Baltimore, the complete documentary package is delivered to and reviewed by the exporter's American Negotiating bank, which then sends the package on and presents it to the Opening bank in Turkey. The Turkish bank checks the documents and, if all is in order, formally "accepts" the Time Drafts. The bank has thus "honored" the credit and will remit $5 million, less an "acceptance" fee, to the exporter via the exporter's bank in 180 days from the B/L date. After securing a promissory note from the importer, the Turkish bank passes the B/L (which serves as title to the Milking Equipment) to the importer who then arranges to pick up the equipment at the Turkish port. It is important to note that if the documents do not conform exactly to the terms given in the L/C, payment will not be made unless and until the Turkish importer agrees to allow the discrepancy.

*Key point*: Before our exporter receives payment, documents must be presented to the importer's bank evidencing that what was agreed upon has actually been shipped. If the documents are correct, the exporter is assured of payment, independent of any action by the importer.

*Side note*: If an importer is concerned that an exporter may not ship what was anticipated, an independent agency may be retained to physically inspect the goods before shipment. Such an agency then issues an inspection certificate vouching that the shipment matches the packing list. Such certificates can be included as part of the documentary package named in the L/C.

The above four steps are critical to commercial success in international trade. The credit risk of the transaction has been absorbed by the banking system (whose business is managing risk). Both the exporter and importer benefit from the commerce, both are protected from their commercial partner's failure to perform, and both have protected their companies' businesses.

## A few additional comments:

The credit underlying this transaction is that of the Turkish importer's bank. Should the American exporter have concern over the soundness of that credit, it can ask its bank, the American Negotiating bank, to "confirm" the Turkish bank's L/C. If the American bank agrees to confirm the Turkish bank's L/C (naturally for a fee), the credit and guarantee of the American bank is added to that of the Turkish bank. This provides an additional level of comfort for the exporter. The American bank then becomes known as the "confirming" bank, and the L/C is now a Confirmed Irrevocable Letter of Credit. The American bank's fee is often taken as a deduction from the ultimate payment to the exporter. A further benefit of such confirmation is that the exporter is now also protected against shortages of hard currency or the imposition of exchange controls by the foreign government after the cargo has shipped.

Now remember that our American exporter agreed to accept payment 180 days after shipping the Milking Equipment. Even though payment is assured, the exporter has to wait six months to receive the funds. Fortunately, when the Turkish bank "accepted" the above Time Draft, it also created what is known as a "Bankers Acceptance" or "B/A," a negotiable money market instrument. Our exporter has the option to hold the B/A for 180 days and then simply receive payment. Or, for cash flow purposes, the exporter may wish to have these funds on hand immediately and will sell this Banker's Acceptance (a receivable) at a discount in the money market. In providing extended payment terms to its Turkish customer, the exporter will likely have built the cost of this discount into its pricing.

# Chapter 4

## *The Basic Hedge on Transaction Exposure*

### THE FORWARD CURRENCY CONTRACT:

Recall in the prior chapter on Trade Documentation that the importer agreed to make payment in US dollars. When one is paid in one's home currency, one has, by definition, no currency exposure. Now, let's say in a similar sale to a dairy cooperative in England, the English insist on paying for the shipment in pounds.

As we know, under a 'dollar-denominated' sale to England, the English importer accepts the risk of currency fluctuations between US dollars and British pounds. If the US dollar appreciates against the pound in the period between the day the Letter of Credit (L/C) was opened and ultimately presented, the US exporter would not care, as payment will be made in US dollars. However, what would happen if the payments were to be in local currency and the L/C was denominated in pounds?

If payment were to be in pounds, our US exporter would now bear the currency exposure risk. If the US dollar appreciates in value against the pound in the time from when the pound—denominated L/C was opened and ultimately paid, each pound received by the US exporter would convert into less US currency. The importer still pays the agreed-upon amount in pounds, but our American exporter receives less than anticipated proceeds in terms of dollars, possibly even creating a loss on the sale.

Fortunately, the banking system is able to limit not only the risks of non-performance and non-payment, but also this currency exposure. To protect itself against a negative currency move, the American exporter could ask its bank to arrange for a forward currency contract. Here the bank would agree to convert the future receipt of pounds into US dollars at a specific exchange rate (for a given volume of currency on a specific date). The US exporter can thus *lock-in* a future exchange rate and be assured of its future dollar receipts. So, if required to accept payment in pounds, our capable American exporter would have worked closely with its bank and then calculated the cost of this forward contract or *cover* into its CIF pricing. There is a very large, deep, and liquid market for such forwards. International bankers are happy to provide advice and a ready market for such contracts and they also build their fees into their forward rate quotes.

## THE FORWARD CURRENCY OPTION:

A variation on the currency forward contract is another hedge called the forward currency option. Our exporter might decide to arrange for a forward currency option instead of a standard forward contract—with the intent of preserving the *option* of being able to choose to either execute a future currency exchange at a set exchange rate—or not—by letting the option lapse. Now why would an exporter not want to lock-in the value of a receivable with a forward cover (a sensible thing to do)? A possible *disadvantage* of a forward cover is that, in eliminating exchange exposure, it also eliminates the opportunity to benefit from a favorable exchange rate move.

The issue here is that while a change in an exchange rate may have a negative impact on a firm's receivable, a currency move in the other direction may present a positive opportunity for that same receivable when converted into one's home currency. In the forward currency contract example above, the future exchange rate is locked-in. The question is, what if our exporter had agreed to accept payment in pounds, and the Pounds had appreciated significantly against the US dollar over the life of the transaction?

With appreciation, each pound that the exporter receives would then be worth more in US dollar terms than before; the revenue from the sale (in US dollar terms) would have increased. Would this be a good thing? Clearly, yes. Revenues and profitability would be greater if the conversion from pounds to dollars were made at the future appreciated spot rate, compared to what would have been received if the exporter had locked-in the receivable with a forward cover.

Our exporter could pay a fee for the *option* to sell (this is known as a *put*) a specific amount of currency for another currency at a prearranged exchange rate (known as the *strike price*) at a future date. The exporter can then either exercise the option or let it lapse on that future date. If the exporter decides to exercise the option, the effect is similar to the currency forward contact and the exporter is protected against the down-side risk of a negative currency move. If the exporter chooses not to exercise the option, the exporter would convert the future pound receivable into its home currency at the future spot rate. If the firm sees it will benefit from exercising the option, it will; if not, it will let the option lapse. This flexibility allows a firm to limit downside risk while preserving upside potential. Remember: a forward contract is just that, a contractual obligation that the firm must make the currency exchange at an agreed upon rate. Such assurance can be a good thing, but one should note that such security may, in a sense, prove to be very "expensive" if the contract obligates the firm to forgo many thousands of US dollar revenues that would be accrued via a future beneficial exchange rate.

*Some comments on currency options:*

Let us say our US exporter purchased a *put* that matures in 12 months on £4,000,000 at a strike price of $1.25/£. Note: at an exchange rate of $1.25/£, this £4,000,000 = US$5,000,000.

In 12 months our exporter has the right, but not the obligation, to sell £4,000,000 and receive $5,000,000. However, unlike forward contracts, options entail greater risks to brokers that sell such options, and they are compensated with up-font fees for selling such *puts*. In our example, the option fee could be $80,000.

If at the 12 month option maturity date the spot rate is below the strike price of 1.25/£, the exporter will exercise its put option; if the future spot rate is above the strike price, the exporter has no incentive to exercise the option and will take the pound receivable and convert it to US dollars at the appreciated future spot rate. The firm thus benefits from the currency move.

For example: if the actual spot rate in 12 months is $1.20/£, then the £4,000,000 receivable would be worth US$4,800,000—well below the hoped-for $5,000,000. So our exporter would exercise* the option and convert the £4,000,000 at the agreed-upon strike price of $1.25/£ for $5,000,000. If the pound had appreciated to $1.30/£, the exporter would not* exercise the option. When the £4,000,000 is received, the exporter would convert the payment into $5,200,000 at the future spot rate (well above the $5,000,000 of a standard forward currency contract). Observe that in both cases, the resulting benefit also covered the cost of the option.

*Note: Whether one exercises the option or not, managers should calculate the true effect of the transaction and reduce the proceeds by the previously paid-up-front option fee (factoring-in the time value of money as well).

# Chapter 5

## Understanding a Resurgent China

*"When the dragon awakes, the whole earth will tremble."*
Napoleon Bonaparte

China calls itself *Tsung-Guo*, the "Middle Kingdom" (or "country in the center of the world"). Interestingly, the Chinese call the United States *Mei-Guo*, "Beautiful Country."

A country of 1.4 billion people (1/5th of humanity) and a member of the BRIC (Brazil, Russia, India, China—those countries that offer the greatest growth opportunities), China presents marketers with the challenge of navigating a land with traditions that go back 3,000 years. This is a high-context culture where business depends upon developing trust and personal connections. As we have mentioned before, such connections are known in China as guān-xì (pronounced: *gwang-she*). Business representatives will not succeed if they presume that they can simply fly in, do a quick-hit presentation and negotiation, close the deal and fly home a hero. Business success in China requires patience and persistence. Multiple trips are required as part of mutual confidence-building, and while this is important in all markets, business arrangements will only flourish where both parties benefit and demonstrate respect for each other. Marketers should not presume that a signed contract in China necessarily provides any real legal recourse. China does not have an independent judiciary or a developed legal tradition. Thus contracts, while nice to look at, are not the endpoint of negotiations, but a signal for the beginning of a relationship. Contracts should be viewed largely as guideposts. At the end of the day, you will succeed only if the relationship succeeds.

The best global managers are culturally sensitive and informed of a target market's history and traditions. Chinese expectations are often low for Western managers' cultural knowledge. Thus, when you exceed expectations and "honor" your host's culture, you and your company will have a much improved chance of success. Effective expatriate managers in the Middle Kingdom understand the broad historic sweep of China's culture and traditions—its ebb and flow with world trade, its eras of engagement followed by eras of isolation.

A good place to start in Chinese history is the ancient northern capital of Xi'an (pronounced: *she-an*), encircled by a 600-hundred year old wall. Xi'an's region is famous for the 2,000 year-old terra cotta soldiers. Xi'an was the wealthy trading terminus of the fabled Silk Road, a caravan trek of 7,000 miles that went all the way to Samarkand, Damascus and Antioch, in modern day Turkey. This is civilization's oldest and longest road, actually called a "fretwork" of trade routes that date back to1,500 B.C.

Along the Silk Road through Central Asia, the great Chinese inventions made their way West. These include printing, gunpowder, the mechanical clock, the spinning wheel and the maritime compass. In addition to its overland trade on the Silk Road, China also was once the world's dominant seafaring power with trade extending through South Asia to the Middle-East and East Africa.

Economic historians note that China's ancient civilization was in many ways ahead of Europe's and its income levels were higher than those in Europe until the 16th century. Yet, over the centuries, that high relative per capita income fell to less than 10% of European levels by the 1970s. From this low point and as part of its historic ebb and flow, China reengaged with the world in 1978, undertook dramatic market-based reforms and experienced the highest and longest sustained growth rates ever seen in world economic history. China ended its extreme poverty and reversed centuries of decline, with per capita incomes now bouncing back to over 20% of those in Europe.

An expatriate manager in China needs to recognize that the Chinese are in reality not just catching up with the West. They are also catching up with their own past as an economic and technological leader. The Chinese know their history and recognize this. Visiting mangers who demonstrate such an understanding of Chinese history will be welcomed and appreciated.

As understanding such a key market as China is important, let us follow some major points in China's history.

Getting back to the northern capital of Xi'an: the city benefited from civilization's longest trade route until the Silk Road was 'cut off' in the mid-15th century when Central Asia splintered into belligerent Turkic and Mongol khanates. At this time, a key event happened in world history. In an astonishing act of self-isolation, the Chinese Ming dynasty, then ruling over the dominant world economy, decided to look inward and close China off from the world. It ordered its heavy merchant fleet back to port and abandoned all trade contacts by land and sea.

Historians seek to explain China's decision to isolate itself by suggesting it was preoccupied with its northern defense and that conservative bureaucrats at the royal court thought the concept of expansion and commercial ventures alien to a Confucian world view. This conservative view pushed China to a revival of a strict agrarian-centered society.

For cultural understanding, visitors to China should be aware that Confucianism is an ancient and deeply embedded Chinese tradition, one that is actually more a way of life than a religion. It encourages a system of ethical and sympathetic relations between people, specifically the relations between ruler and subject, parent and child, older and younger siblings, husband and wife, friend and friend. Confucianism supports the view that following such a system of relationships through etiquette and ritual will lead to a harmonious society.

The ruling Ming dynasty recognized that it had achieved high levels of sophistication in the economy, arts, society and politics, and this promoted a belief among the Chinese elite that they had the most satisfactory civilization on earth and that nothing foreign was needed or welcome.

A famous date in Chinese history is **1434**, the date of China's last trade voyage. At roughly the same time, Spain and Portugal began to build their empires and Columbus' voyage intended for the Orient led to other discoveries. The Portuguese pioneered sea routes around Africa. Europe developed while China lay dormant. The economic weight of the world shifted.

This isolationist theme continued through to the modern era, including the rule of the infamous Ching dynasty "Dowager Empress" Tzu Hsi in the late 1800s. Your Chinese business counterparts will be fully aware of how she wasted China's resources and cared little for the outside world. She also did not move to rebuff the expansionist Western and Japanese colonial powers. These powers then created independent zones (called Concessions) in China's coastal cities and controlled much of China's commerce and trade.

Another important date to the Chinese is **1898.** At this time, many of China's best educated and patriotic students were influenced by nearby Japan's successful transformation into a modern and industrialized country. Japan was also demonstrating that the people of Asia were fully capable of standing up to and competing with the Western colonial powers. Looking across the Straits of Japan, the students saw that Japan's 1868 Meiji Restoration had moved Japan to become a modern state in one generation. Chinese students looked to similarly reform China's archaic system of governance and looked for their country to again play an important and active role in the world. They pushed for what became known as the 100-day Program of Reforms. The Dowager Empress had the reformers arrested and killed (echoes of the Chinese government's confrontation with students in Beijing's Tiananmen Square in 1989). China's opportunity for reform was lost, and her position as a weak and colonized country continued.

After the death of the Dowager Empress, China's famous "Last Emperor," PuYi, came to power but was shortly thereafter deposed in **1911** in what is known as the Chinese National Revolution. Into the power vacuum, Dr. Sun Yat-sen was elected by provincial representatives to be the first President of the Republic of China. He had hopes of a reunited modern China taking its rightful place among the community of nations. Dr. Sun is a fascinating historic figure and considered by many Chinese as the father of modern China, a status similar to that of America's George Washington. Dr. Sun was born near Hong Kong, had part of his education in Hawaii and even became a US citizen. Chinese tradition notes that he studied US history and was intrigued by Lincoln's words in the Gettysburg Address: *Government of the people, by the people, for the people.* Dr. Sun saw these words as especially relevant to the establishment of a modern society in China after 2,000 years of imperial rule. When he returned to China, Dr. Sun promoted his Three Principles of the People:

*Nationalism*—the desire to reestablish sovereignty; China then was still occupied by colonial powers.
*Democracy*—the need to replace autocratic dynasties with representative government.
*Socialism*—the wish to structure society for the benefit of all the people, not just an elite class.

The major coastal city of Shanghai was still divided by the colonial powers into their own Concessions, and there was great resentment against this continued occupation. Even today, one can meet those that grew up in Shanghai with memories of being forced to bow when passing a Japanese soldier or being insulted by signs on park entrances that said "Chinese & Dogs Not Permitted." In addition to friction with the foreign Concessions, the early 20th century was a time of great turmoil as such a large and diverse country as China was extremely difficult to govern. China fell into civil chaos; local warlords controlled much of the interior. By 1925 Dr. Sun Yat-sen, the founder of the republic had died. Seeing an opportunity to expand its own empire, Japan took advantage of China's weak government and occupied Manchuria in 1931 and then moved to overrun much of China by 1937.

As is well known, at the end of World War II, imperial Japan was forced to return to its home islands. With the Japanese departure, China experienced great internal strife between Chinese "Nationalists" and "Communists." These factions had once united against the common Japanese foe, but in the post-war era, when they competed for power, the country fell into civil war. In **1949** the Nationalists were defeated and retreated to Formosa (now called Taiwan) where they set up an independent government called the Republic of China (ROC). There the exiles developed a strong market-based economy that is one of the 'economic tigers' of Asia. While some on the island hope to retain their own national identity, many in China and Taiwan look forward to eventual reunification.

The Communist leader, Mao Zedong, was now victorious and able to claim responsibility for having achieved one of Dr. Sun's principal goals, that of *Nationalism,* by finally reestablishing Chinese independence with a nationally unified government. For this success, Mao remains honored today. However, this unity was achieved through ruthless state and party control. China remained difficult to govern. To retain his hold on power, Mao relied on mob rule and, by the 1960s, launched what was called the Cultural Revolution. He also worked to develop a personality cult around himself as the "Great Leader." And, like emperors before him, Mao closed China's borders and the country looked inward.

In China, you will still meet survivors of Mao's 1966-1976 Cultural Revolution, a process that turned Chinese society upside down. A constant in Chinese life until the Cultural Revolution had been Confucianism, and Mao tried to uproot this cultural foundation. Mao's attempt at "permanent revolution" disrupted China's development and ended the education of a whole generation. The Cultural Revolution was xenophobic (perhaps understandable in the context of the colonial experience) and included brutal persecution of those that had any contact with the world beyond China. This was a time of mass terror in which many millions died.

Mao also initiated a program in 1958 called the Great Leap Forward. He sought to modernize China on the Soviet industrial model and instructed peasants to stop planting crops and start producing steel using tiny and ineffective neighborhood furnaces. The result was the production of a lot of worthless "pig iron," but not food. Historians calculate that more than 38 million then died in the greatest famine in history. Overall, historians calculate that 70 million perished under Mao's rule—all in peacetime.

Much of Mao's legacy of autocratic rule, some say an imperial legacy, remains. Mao's picture hangs above the entrance to the famous Forbidden City, looking down on Beijing's Tiananmen Square, the political heart of China. In the same square is Mao's mausoleum, referred to by some Chinese as a modern-day emperor's tomb. Mao's legacy is a sensitive subject, and visitors to China would be wise not to comment on the hardships of Mao's rule. The Chinese know these all too well. Nonetheless, Mao remains a potent symbol of China's reunification and sovereignty.

After Mao died in 1976, a veteran political insider in the Communist Party of China, Deng Xiaoping (who had been 'denounced and purged' during the Cultural Revolution) promptly instituted market reforms and opened the country to world trade. China's communal farming system, a structure that had been imposed by Mao, was dismantled and several hundred million farm households suddenly had market incentives to produce. Food yields boomed; there are no more famines in China. This important liberalization resulted in efficiency in the farm sector and freed up labor for the manufacturing export sector, a key driver of Chinese economic growth to this day. To support manufacturing and engage more fully with the world, China opened numerous tariff-free Special Economic Zones (SEZs), many overlapping what had been the colonial Concessions. Economic performance in the zones was phenomenal. These zones have evolved into major business centers. Since the reforms began, China has become the world's most successful economy, growing at an average annual rate of 8%.

From a cultural perspective, the Chinese are not proud of the last 100 years—though, given China's many thousand years of history, the last century is truly seen as a "drop in the ocean." This is definitely the view from Beijing (the seat of political power) in terms of its long-term decision-making mentality. It also is important for expatriate managers to be sensitive to the tension between Beijing and Shanghai (the great commercial center on China's southeast coast and major source of Beijing's tax revenues). The business community in Shanghai views itself as smarter and more dynamic than the government bureaucrats in Beijing. A local manager in Shanghai commented to the author, "The sky is very high and the Emperor is far away." This reflects the more independent and freewheeling world view of Shanghai versus Beijing's central government attempts at control.

With all the above, you now have a good introduction to understanding the China market. Readers who are effective in China may someday be referred to as a "*China-hand*," an informal but solid credential.

To managers who ask the question, "Does all this cultural stuff really matter?" The answer is a resounding "Yes." For example, the regional manager for a major pharmaceutical company spent over a year in southern China developing a JV to start up local production and distribution of medicine. To complete the deal, a high government official needed to grant approval, and, as a matter of protocol, the CEO of the pharmaceutical firm was invited to fly to China to complete the formalities with a signing ceremony. Though a capable manager in the US and well meaning, the CEO proceeded to demonstrate that he hadn't cared enough to have even a minimal understanding of Chinese culture, and, through naïveté, even insulted the government official. The Chinese politely backed away from the project. The CEO flew home clueless, still wondering what had happened. It took the capable regional manager over a year to get the project back on track.

Finally, understand that your Chinese business counterparts will be justifiably proud of their country's achievements. Effective expatriate managers make a point of honoring the Chinese people's success in world trade. China's economy holds great promise; an economy that today exports not only toys but also biomass steam boilers to Peru and wind turbines to Texas; an economy that is already the second largest in the world and on a path to eclipse the US in total GDP. China already has the most modern city in the world, Shanghai. When you visit there, you will see the driving heart of modern capitalist China, a China no longer isolationist, but open and engaged with the world. As we noted before, China should not simply be seen as catching up with the West. It is a country returning to a role it once played, that of a leading global player economically, technologically, politically and culturally.

# Chapter 6

## Business Ethics in a Diverse World

This concluding chapter is a brief but important reflection on an issue that faces all managers operating in today's dynamic global environment. The issue is ethics, and, specifically, how managers face the daily challenges of corruption.

Yes, it is biblical that we live in a fallen world, and we certainly do. We also live in a wonderful mosaic of cultures, each with a distinct way of looking at the world, often very different from our own. An interesting quote comes from the 17th century mathematician and philosopher Pascal:

> *"There are truths on this side of the Pyrenees that are falsehoods on the other."*

Any good instructor in cross-cultural communication will stress that in working internationally, whether in the corporate, diplomatic or not-for-profit NGO worlds, we need to be aware of our own biases and our own ethnocentrism. Ethnocentrism is the tendency for managers to be parochial; to believe in the superiority of their own group or culture; to think that the home-country's way of doing things is better, and that home-country managers are inherently more intelligent and effective than foreign mangers. A global manager should seek to avoid imposing his or her own cultural attitudes and approaches on others. The best global managers have developed an appreciation for diversity and in a very pragmatic way see cultural differences as a resource, not a limitation. So it is not surprising that high value is placed on managers who are well traveled and are at-ease in foreign environments. There is an appropriate quote by Mark Twain:

*"Catch the trade winds in your sails. Explore, Dream, Discover,*
*Travel is fatal to prejudice, bigotry, and narrow-mindedness."*

Openness is a necessary foundation for global managers, but when one operates commercially in the world, one also sees corruption in every society and on every continent.

In Africa there is the impoverished country of Nigeria. Yes Nigeria, a country that produces more oil each day than Kuwait—a country where 80% of the oil revenue accrues to just 1% of the population, where former dictator Sani Abacha looted not tens of millions, not hundreds of millions, but over $3 billion during his rule. This is a country where its people survive on less than a dollar a day.

As we mentioned before, in China there is the term guān-xì meaning at one level "relationship" and "connections" and at a further level, "influence." As there is little faith in the niceties of legal documents in China, the reality is that without the correct guān-xì with high government officials, doing business is problematic. A report by the Stockholm School of Economics notes that the costs of such guān-xì can double a firm's anticipated costs of doing business.

And just so that we do not delude ourselves about our own culture or ethnocentric superiority, we do not have to go far to hear about the malfeasance of far too many governors of American states—from New York to Connecticut to New Jersey and on to Mr. Blagojevich, the fourth Illinois governor to be jailed in four decades.

A point in this connection is that Chinese mayors convicted of corruption aren't necessarily sentenced to do time, they may even be sentenced to death. However, due to guān-xì, the sentence is not necessarily carried out.

So if corruption is part of our world, and it is, we are led to the question, "How does one operate?" In getting things done overseas, sometimes *baksheesh,* or, to use a more benign word, a gratuity is asked for. In other countries this is called *grease,* or in Nigeria, *dash.* In many countries, this is an everyday part of living. In India, there are almost standard rates for it. If you want a phone line to your house, you can have it next week (that is if you pay the foreman a set charge of 5,000 rupees) or you can wait a year. Also, after you pay your taxes, the municipal clerk is supposed to give you a voucher showing that you have paid. However, for that voucher, you need to give him a gratuity on top of the taxes. If you do not pay, the voucher will be lost somewhere in the bureaucracy, and, as you will be unable to prove you've paid your taxes, you will be in violation of the law.

Interestingly, there are times when you can legally pay gratuities, or what some call "facilitating payments." You may well have heard of the Foreign Corrupt Practices Act (FCPA) of 1977 which was a response to significant bribes that Lockheed paid to Japanese government officials in the 1970s. The Act is quite strict and at times placed US exporters at a disadvantage compared to other companies from other countries such as France, that didn't operate under such restrictions. Today, the OECD (Organization for Economic Cooperation and Development) seeks to coordinate payment rules among countries, and a convention was signed in 1997 among the 33 major trading nations. Per the US Department of Justice, the FCPA focuses on the *purpose* of the payment instead of the particular duties of the official receiving the payment or promise of payment.

The FCPA contains an explicit exception to the bribery prohibition for "facilitating payments" regarding "routine governmental action." The statute lists the following examples: obtaining permits, licenses, or other official documents, processing governmental papers such as visas and work permits, providing police protection, mail pick-up and delivery, providing phone service, power and water supply, loading and unloading cargo, protecting perishable products, and scheduling. The FCPA allows these exceptions as long as a payment is "low-level," does not provide a competitive business advantage, and as long as the gratuity is for a service that the foreign government employee's job is to do anyway (such as a customs officer rubber stamping entry documents today versus next month). These are permissible.

Some would say that such payments show that one is simply adapting to a country's local norms, is not showing an ethnocentric bias, and is not seeking to dictate, through some form of cultural imperialism, how another culture should operate. Some others would say that not operating "in the real world" would simply be naive and one would be one of Mark Twain's *Innocents Abroad*.

However, my corporate experience and conversations with many global managers have shown me that senior managers make the point that in dealings with leaders in both industry and government, when the issue of effective leadership comes up, few qualities are mentioned with greater force or frequency than integrity. It is the social cement of the leader-follower dynamic. Making a financial or personal investment in someone is a leap of faith and trust. It is where leadership meets reality. Most investors, company CEOs, and government officials place a premium on honesty and trustworthiness in making decisions on investments or partnerships. Global managers know enough to walk away from potentially lucrative deals when a sense of trust has not been developed.

If there is no trust or integrity, success is at best temporary and limited. Lasting success is built on repeated interaction and repeated business transactions. One tends to do business with those whom one trusts and have had success with before. "Cheat me once, shame on me; cheat me twice and the entire industry will know about you." That is a truth. It also is a truth that once your credibility is put in question, rebuilding it is almost impossible.

Ethics and integrity go beyond adherence to local laws governing your industry or business. Ethics go beyond borders and cultures and are aligned with a higher universal truth and good. Ethics should not be a Risk-Benefit calculation, i.e., adjusting the degree of compliance to the benefits or risks involved.

I have traveled in over 60 countries, and I would submit that there is a remarkably universal code of ethics—a sense of right and wrong—across cultures and across borders. The Explanation in Luther's Small Catechism says it well, "*When God created people, He wrote the law on their hearts.*"

At a fundamental level, all people recognize that graft and corruption are wrong. The real question is actually one of degree; that is, the level of tolerance by a person or society for wrong doing. So when an expatriate manager seeks to act with integrity, I dismiss the notion that he or she is an agent of western cultural imperialism trying to impose his or her own version of ethics on others. Now, this is a nice, but is it *real world*? In an often corrupt world, can a business act ethically and prosper? Or from a more 'liberal' perspective, are businesses in market economies even capable of acting ethically?

The answer to these questions is yes, and it's a *real world* yes.

A friend of mine was the European Director of a major pharmaceutical company based in Brussels, Belgium. Those that are involved in global trade will know that Belgium is sometimes referred to as the '*Sicily of the North*' and that is not a term of endearment.

The Director's company was importing an important drug, and the shipments were being held up in customs by officials looking to shake down the company. The Director took the issue to the highest levels in Government, the Ministry of the Interior and the Ministry of Finance. They listened and smiled but did not act. The Director then put a hold on further shipments to doctors and hospitals, which understandably created a groundswell of concern in the medical community. The press picked up on this and shamed the government ministries into clearing the shipments. Ethical calls like this are clearly not the "road of least resistance" or the way of "getting along." But they can lead to change. Today Belgian officials know better than to try and shake down that company again. The lesson is that when one's position is clear, i.e., that corruption and collusion are not 'common practice', then it will not be attempted.

Another example is with the systemic corruption in the former communist states in Eastern Europe and Russia – corruption to the extent that sanguine global managers often decide not to play this game and walk away from doing business there. In working in these markets, this same Director required not just employees, but all vendors and licensees to sign and adhere to a code of ethics. There was a time when the manager's approach was not taken seriously, and he was ignored. He then fired some very senior people. He fired the company director for Central Europe; he fired the company director for Russia; he even fired the in-house general counsel. Was this easy? Of course not. Did it disrupt business? Yes, but in the short term. The manager correctly believed that being known for an ethical approach to business is a long-tern competitive advantage, not a disadvantage.

We also note that such an ethical approach is not unique. We can look at the example of PepsiCo which has a strict code of ethics and conduct for its dealings around the world. A friend and former PepsiCo VP for International Marketing talks about how double standards simply don't work. In addition to ethical behavior simply being the right thing to do, the down-side exposure of wrongdoing can have devastating PR and commercial implications. This senior manager notes that codes of ethics can drive managers to make tough choices in global markets, even putting one's company at a competitive disadvantage when competitors behave in an unethical but locally acceptable way. And while it can make a manager's life harder in the short term, over time, in that VP's experience, sound business principles and ethics pay off. The VP also notes that we do not need to be cultural boors or insensitive. In some countries (e.g., Saudi Arabia or Egypt), gift giving is very important, and refusing a gift can cause offense. So a creative solution might be to accept the gift, declare it to your employer and then auction it off at a charity event.

Both managers I have mentioned view ethical compromise as a slippery slope.

Now more than ever, the world needs both highly competent and ethical international managers. Ethical behavior must come as a basic conviction of principle. If it is governed by an inner sense of right and wrong, a sense of fairness and human compassion, it will guide us all, not only as a way of doing business but also as a way of life. As a global manager I greatly respect says to each of his employees, "*Everything in life is temporary except two things, your integrity and your family. Jeopardize either by unethical behavior and you will never get them back.*"

# Addendum—Common Trade Abbreviations used in this Text

www.ingramcontent.com/pod-product-compliance
Lightning Source LLC
Chambersburg PA
CBHW020339290526
45785CB00005B/2094